BREATHE THE DEEP WATERS OF LOVE

A Dive Into Loss, Grief, Afterlife Connection, Self-Love and Living Life Forward

Becki Koon

PRAISE FOR BREATHE THE DEEP WATERS OF LOVE

Becki is a bright-light in our world, and a brave and beautiful writer. Her latest book is a powerfully intimate, revealing testament to love after death, and the choice we can make to live, even when life seems in its darkest hour. Prepare to be inspired and touched.

Lee Harris, Author, Teacher and Intuitive Guide

I had not yet met Becki when I read her book, 20 Days Changed Everything: A Love Story Moving Through Conscious Death to Afterlife Connection. However, her writing was so exquisitely descriptive, honest, authentic and moving, I felt as if I knew Becki-almost at a soul level. Her words, her spiritual passions and work as a healer, matched my own. When our divinely timed connection was made, I knew this friendship had come at a critical point in both our life's journey.

This book describes an enduring love and one incredible woman's journey through the valley of death to the open field of possibilities on this earth plane. I was honored to walk through this valley, In Presence with her, through hypnosis, energy healing, channeling and mediumship. It was all I could do, to bring through my own healing gifts in alignment with Becki's divine plan and not my own. For I selfishly and desperately wanted to keep her anchored to earth. Month's later, God's healing on her behalf was reciprocated, as she ministered to me while my 39 year marriage, gasped its last breath. Love came full circle.

This book is that full circle offering of hope through any struggles you might be experiencing, or have experienced. You will be led to a profound understanding of the power of love and the force of healing that exists to choose your own destiny. It is all love. Breathe it in by taking in the depths of this book. You will be forever changed as I was, as you witness a life lived deeply, breathing beauty into every moment.

Barbara Rose
Spiritual Energy Healer, Hypnotherapist, Licensed Minister, Channeler, Medium
www.sparksoftheDivine.com

I can honestly say, after working with thousands of patients, Becki Koon's exploration of conventional, naturopathic, and esoteric modalities of healing goes unparalleled. A truly unique story!

Dr. Mark Kelley, ND, LAc
Three Rivers Natural Medicine

Becki takes us on a journey, passing through present and past. Detailing her way of finding healing in modalities many may not be familiar with, and few have probably tried. She is showing us with bravery there are so many ways to live and bring light into your life, even when that life has thrown you curveballs. A wonderfully intimate replay that spans time and space, and allows us to realize the importance of how our connections can affect our health and beyond. Becki's tangible experiences are an invitation for everyone reading to dig deeper into what they, themselves, are capable of, and to move forward in those capabilities, both for healing themselves from illness and finding joy in life through connections.

Hillary Sargent
Owner Two Poppies Apothecary, Nutritional Herbalist, Bioresonance, BodyTalk
www.twopoppiesapothecary.com

Becki weaves together many of the components needed for true healing. Coming through cancer is not easy and requires all the tools a person has access to. I love that she is able to articulate the subtler aspects of this process with such clarity. It is my hope that this book can serve as a model for how others can walk themselves out of danger the way that Becki did.

Dr. Mathew Schlechten, ND
Naturopathic Doctor, Cancer Recovery Specialist

Becki has again opened and shared her beautiful heart with us in this, her second, amazing book. She speaks in depth of her journey to hope and purpose through some of the more difficult and potentially overwhelming struggles we humans can have on our planet. She has chosen to help others with skills both innate and learned through many classes and books, as well as through the experiences, emotions, and decisions she describes in her books. Becki radiates love, intuition, understanding, compassion, and non-judgment with family, friends, acquaintances, clients, students, as well as in her writing. We all benefit from contact with her loving and vibrant life force.

Adele Lewis, Author
Listening To Animals

Becki paints a picture with words that touch us at a very deep level, a place many have never gone before – existing in a state of unconditional love, contributing to healing of the body, mind, and soul. As soul mates, she and Jack learned how to shift in and out of frequencies to continue to communicate and be together after death. Jack helped encourage and support Becki into purpose and healing, supporting her as her 'wing-man' for what she came to do in this lifetime.

This is where healing begins. By remembering we are powerful healers through love, laughter, energy, natural healthy treatments, and by being with others who are of a similar energetic frequency, those who are choosing to rise. Becki describes her healing process with such precision, it is a guide for growing, healing, and being here to explore what it is we came on the earth to do.

Love never dies, it only remains as a state of being. This is where Becki found healing, through the heart.

Jane Berryhill, M.S.
Clinical Counselor/Biofeedback Therapist
Minds in Motion, Steamboat Springs, Colorado

DEDICATION

This book is dedicated to my beloved Jack, who eternally shares in my journey, and to my family and friends who were ever present, holding my physical body, mind, and soul as I walked the path between life, death and love. Thank you God for the breath of life you have gifted me.

TABLE OF CONTENTS

FOREWORD

Geoffrey Clow with Georgie Bailey

Canberra, Australia December 2022

When Becki Koon asked me if I would be interested in writing a foreword for her upcoming book, I was somewhat surprised. My heart was also touched, but I was still taken aback by the honor. Three months prior to when Becki asked me, I didn't even know who Becki was. I didn't know that she wrote a best selling book, *20 Days Changed Everything*.

You see, I was just a guy living in Australia, doing his part to live a good life with a wonderful lady. During the course of eight years or so, we developed a deep and meaningful love bond that was fun, safe, supportive, and uplifting. It was filled with kindness, laughter, adventure, and the grounded assurance of unshakeable, unbreakable love. There we were, happy in love, happy in love, until one of us died all too soon. Georgie died from complications following routine muscle biopsy surgery. She developed a deep vein thrombosis that traveled from her leg to her lungs. This blocked her pulmonary artery, causing her to have a massive heart attack. This attack took her away from us. There are no words to describe how devastating this moment was.

In the moments after Georgie died, deep grief took over and held me hostage. It numbed me and dumbed me to the very recesses of my soul. Raw, ripped open, torn apart, and broken. Our lives, my future, and our future all shattered into pieces. The pieces would have been picked up, but there were none to pick up, they vaporized, every single one of them, gone forever.

My heart was gripped tight by pain, my body awash with torment that erupted through me. The agony of realization it was the end of the road for such a beautiful soul who was just trying to get through an autoimmune disease that was slowly attacking every cell in her body and killing her. We were trying to help her through treatment, hoping we could turn her immune system around to stop treating her as the enemy.

It was a time when all my senses were numb. Nothing tasted like anything. I couldn't drink enough water to quench my thirst. Everything around me seemed to be moving too fast. Everything seemed like a threat. Even the small things I thought I could count on I questioned, but suddenly I could feel Georgie. I could feel her as if she was with me. It was feelings that were imbued with the same essence of the deep love bond we created in our physical time together. I thought I was going crazy. The only thing I could sense was her. Was I crazy? Was my mind playing tricks on me? I was yearning for her. Of course I was. I was wishing that what was happening, wasn't happening.

In between all of it, I was receiving impulses that came through clear. Georgie pointed me to Lee Harris. Well, I thought, "Okay, I'm just here by myself, nobody is going to see I'm acting on a received impulse from my dead beloved. I don't know who Lee Harris is but I'll just jump online and have a look."

I jumped online and found Lee's website and went into his Portal Community which seemed vast and impressive. The first thing I came to was an interview that Lee was doing with a lady called Becki. And even though it was playing, I wasn't really taking in what was being discussed because another impulse came through to me, which was, there's a book and it's important. So, I searched online quickly and put Becki's name in Google. I saw a book, 20 *Days Changed Everything*, and it seemed right to buy the book. I didn't read reviews, I didn't see who Becki was. I just thought, I'm running with these impulses because it feels like Georgie is guiding me.

At the same time, I was wondering again, was I crazy? How could my dead beloved be talking to me, sending me messages? And, not only was I questioning how could she be talking to me, but the feeling I received felt imbued with this same love essence we shared in life. What sort of magic was this?

Becki's book arrived 24 hours after I ordered it. I then received another impulse that came through to me, which was "start reading from halfway, you're not ready for the first part". The first part of the book, from what I understand (I haven't been able to read it yet) is where Becki loved her partner, Jack, from his cancer diagnosis through to his death, and to his transition. I picked up on the second part of the book, where Becki talks about the connection that continued with Jack after he passed. And, her expression of the deep love that continued.

Around the same time, I received another impulse. I'm not quite sure if I'm using right word to describe what happens. It was just a thought form that came between the cracks with clarity amidst the all consuming deep grief. I was to contact Becki. "Contact Becki, it's important." I thought, "Oh well, same thing again. I've got nothing to lose here. I've lost the most wonderful person in the world. Why not?" And obviously, all sorts of other thoughts were running through my head. Why would a best selling author want to talk to me? I'm just a guy on the other side of the planet, living his life who's lost because he's lost his most beloved.

So, I sent an email and explained that this is where I was up to and how I couldn't quite understand how I found her because I actually didn't, Georgie guided me. I started to share what I felt when I was reading her book, it was heart breaking and also soothing at the same time. Becki's expression of deep love and connection for Jack was so similar and resonated throughout me, my body. I found myself nodding all the way through. It was so similar to the love that Georgie and I created. In one sense, it felt like recognition, it was deeply tender, very relatable and the tears flowed. But, in another sense, I couldn't understand why it was so similar. Georgie had also left me a book about her life story and other channeled thought forms were coming through. It felt like I was to do something with Georgie's book. So, I sent a part of it to Becki and started to work with Becki on what it all meant.

I have such deep gratitude for Becki and her work for many reasons. She is the same pure expression of divine love I witnessed with my Georgie, Becki too sees through the eyes of Source or the eyes of whichever God you prefer. I am in awe of her courage and her bravery as what she shares, in this, her newest book, is deeply intimate, personal, and profoundly moving. It's an expression of love that is woven and told in a multilayer of the not often talked about subject of loving someone when they're dead.

On another different level, it's a powerful portrayal of a woman who is also confronted by her own challenges of life or death. It's an astonishing journey by a truly remarkable person. Becki's courageousness in putting her very personal story out there is to be acknowledged given that not everyone has this wider and deep understanding of love, death, and connecting and communicating with people when they've died or transitioned. Her self-love back to vibrant life is commendable.

There's another significant part of Becki's writings in this book which is the mastery of the channels she shares from Jack. To me, it's a whole other level of understanding, a unique perspective of divine male energy that's being shared through Becki who has been able to tell it in an attainable way, in a way that resonates and connects while at the same time, for me, soothes and uplifts. It also never strays from what deep love is, it is deep, tender, and moving. And, in all that gloriousness, in parts also humanly painful.

Working with Becki has helped me get out of my own way, to be able to sense the connection, the ongoing connection I have with Georgie. It is incredibly precious to me. It's a connection that I can't maintain all the time because I'm human, I get the "sads" as I miss her terribly. But when I can let myself calibrate to the right space we connect, she flows through with a warm vibrating energy.

The other aspect I enjoy with Becki is she's not trying to be anything else but her authentic self. She's not trying to fix the world or anyone else. It has to be admired that she is comfortable being Becki, a lady who sits in eternal divine love, who has access to Source Energy or a God of your choosing, and other Spirit energy. It's been my experience that she is a conduit between those energies and us humans. I found working with Becki helps to shorten the space between the different energy fields, between where Georgie is and where I am. Reading Becki's expression of love, care and kindness has reminded me of how beautiful deep love and continuing connection is. Importantly, Becki has helped me realize I'm not crazy. I'm just a guy who loved a very special lady that died, a guy who is still loving that lady where she is.

It's early days for me but I'm learning that I too can continue to Breathe The Deep Waters Of Love. I know you can too. Becki is showing us all how.

PREFACE

I am filled with immense gratitude in being able to share this book with the world. Actually, it was inevitable this book would form, take shape, and have life breathed into its existence. My beloved Jack, who passed from this world on September 24, 2019, told me we would be writing a second book. Our first book together, *20 Days Changed Everything - A Love Story Moving Through Conscious Death To Afterlife Connection*, became a bestseller. I could not foresee the impact it would have with readers. In the final chapter of the book, Jack channeled through me that we were not done, there would be more to share. He alluded to the fact another book would be coming and I felt it too. But what would it be about?

What you, the reader, now have in your hands is the result of an exploration into the meaning behind Jack's prophetic message. I would explore the many facets of love. I was catapulted into a deep dive within my own soul in a way I was not prepared for nor one I would have chosen to explore in the way you will discover.

I am honored you chose to pick up this book, to dive into the deep waters with me. I want you to walk side-by-side with me as we discover new awarenesses, uncover the meaning of life not only for your own journey into love and all of its expressions but for the benefit of the collective conscious energy we are all a part of.

Jack was right. There was another book to write. What I did not understand was the fortitude it would require to find the form, how it would take shape, and the magnitude of focused breathing it would demand to find its way to life. The blessing is that I am still present on this planet to share it. One possibility was the book would never be written but then, divine providence found its way to manifest, this book, *Breathe The Deep Waters Of Love*, was meant to exist.

Jack and I are still on a journey together, our afterlife connection is an unending love story that continues to grow, expand, shift, and evolve for both us, as I alone, here on the earth plane continue to do as well. While Jack is with me in this second book, it is much more a of human story, a human who bridges realms and finds her way to breathing life into some of the most challenging aspects of being a soul embodied in physicality.

Thank you for joining us as we dive into the deep waters of love together. We offer this book to the world with complete surrender to the destiny of divine love for all.

Blessings to you,
Becki and Jack
Step Stone Studio 2022

INTRODUCTION

Becki Journal Entry July 2021

How can I express the depths of love that is beyond this world, beyond this time, beyond this dimension, the love that spans the universe, hearts beating as one. in one breath, one movement, in one moment, intertwined in an embrace of timeless ecstatic connection?

How can I ever let go of that kind of manifestation in the physical, when the other half of me left the earth plane? How can I trust that life will evolve? How can I trust that I will move on in some fashion, the ache that chokes me becoming a distant memory instead of an ever-present reality? How can I let go of my longing for you, my love? I don't know how to do this very well, this part of my heart moving forward. I can't seem to see past you, my love of you, my want of you physically here.

I want to extend a welcome to you, the reader, to the journey taken with me as you read the words that spilled onto the page while I recapitulated a year in my life, my life unique to me yet a part of the walk we all take to self-awareness, expansion, love, and LIFE. As I contemplated writing this book, I wondered what it would look like; what I would share that hadn't already been written in *20 Days Changed Everything: A Love Story Moving Through Conscious Death to Afterlife Connection.* And yet, I felt the pulling on my heart to explore more, to expand more, to honor Jack's message in our first book that we were not done. My beloved in the afterlife, with whom I remain connected, knew there was to be another book. But I had no idea of the events that would catapult me into questioning life once more, challenging me to make a choice, actually many choices that were life altering. Again, I found myself exposing aspects of an incredible life journey through words that could only point to the experience, hoping in some fashion, by my sharing, that readers would find themselves within the pages, connected to me, understanding we are all amazing souls surfing and crashing with the waves of our humanity. I was asking the questions, "Would others want to ride the waves through the deep waters of love with me; breathe in the essence of loss, grief, afterlife connection, self-love, and living life forward? Would others find a spark of recognition for themselves through my raw and often challenging sharing? Would others find hope in the messages coming through me? Will others feel the honoring of life I now experience with every breath I take?"

My answers were guided by a wisdom greater than myself, a hand that channeled the energy of spirit, the energy of compassion, the essence of divine love imbued with that wisdom.

You were so unique, my love. I could feel your desire of me when your hand touched my skin, your energy pulsing through to my body, signaling in a touch your heart's desire. Feeling you make love to me, only it was a divine love mixed with your human desire of me, my heart, my soul. I find my want of you surfacing now in my moment of vulnerability, my moment of fatigue from an intense journey the last few months. I am still raw. My heart feels open, jagged, and sore.

And yet, my strength is to see beyond the physical scars, the emotional wounds, to the soul connection we now share, my love, the unending love we experience. As you told me, "This is the dance that we do. Life. Love. Death. Divine connection. We've done this dance for eons, over and over again, as we dance the evolution of our souls' journey!" Trust in that kind of devotional love, I hear you say. "OK, I will," I respond. I have no choice but to commit to this life, this journey, this story as it has unfolded. If I could breathe life back into you, I would. But then the course of events would change. We would not be stepping into our contract, our destiny. The journey we know, the one we have taken over and over again, two souls on the wheel of experiencing love at its deepest and widest breadth, the over lighting energy of love that animates everything in the universe, the I AM that I AM, God source and expansion.

When I can step back and see the bigger picture, I understand. I can breathe into the magic of what we share, the sheer power of divine love manifest into form. We are blessed, my love. But it is the very human aspect of me, the flesh and blood Becki, the body that feels the soft touch of a hand in desire, that misses your form, your beautiful body. I adored your body, the way you moved. I watched you more than you knew and when you were playing music, at one with the sound and vibration, I was in awe. I found myself in rapture from the sheer beauty of seeing you move, hearing you create, express, love, the only way you and that body could. I was enamored with how you would move your head as we were making love or you were listening to a piece of beautiful music that moved your soul. I find myself moving my head in a similar way as I listen to music that moves me, as if I am channeling an aspect of you through my body. I close my eyes and my heart warms with the vision I see, the subtle energy exchange a delicious memory to treasure.

My love, you taught me to feel. To feel deeply. To experience life deeply. To become more than I am in every now moment. You carried such a love of the small moments, the special nature of life. I gaze at the clouds looking for you to be there. I stare at the moon and feel the soft skin of your neck under my gentle kiss. I hear you when I'm not paying attention, reminding me, making me smile. How can it be that I am here now without the other half of myself? The fulfilling of a contract we did not understand until you were leaving your body. To know great love is to also know great loss, the two sides or facets of the same expression, the energy intwined in a celestial dance that creates bliss and excruciating heartache.

I am reminded of a spirit channeling that came through to me. To be able to alchemize energy and transform it, you must know it. In other words, you have to have lived it and understand it at a core level. When you have lived it, you have this transformational capacity to shift it, to change it, move it, and alchemize it into something new. This is our journey. This is my journey. Life is mine to experience with all its many colors, vibrations, emotions, expressions, experiences, and loves. As is yours.

In meditation one day, I was given the name of this book, *Breathe the Deep Waters of Love*. It was clear the metaphor of water was being shown to me in the same context as love, two of the greatest powers we know, one of earthly plane and one of spiritual plane, the spiritual heart within all that is. The versions of water as life became the context within which the second book Jack and I were to write became clearer, less murky, even as my life unfolded.

This book is written in the timeline of events over a one-year span. I have included many journal entries along the way, giving you a glimpse into my life, my illness, my process, my own brush with death and my growing and expanding into a newer version of myself. My hope is you will find connection in the sharing, the vulnerable heart-opening offered on these pages. Perhaps you will find within you your own strength to move through great loss and grief, to love yourself through intense illness and questioning life, to know you are not alone and there are others who share your tears of sadness as well as your tears of joy.

As energetic beings, we do not live in isolation even if we do not have anyone with us physically. We are multi-dimensional humans learning to access greater and greater realms of possibility while navigating our deeply human reality. Our energetic heart centers are coming online in ways we never dreamed possible, and as a result, the gamut of our human emotional waters can quench the yearning thirst of our soul like never before.

Can we learn to breathe in the deep waters of love in all its forms and expressions?

That is the quest.

Chapter 1

THE WAKE

March 2021

"My love, this type of sacred love, this divine union, IS the universe. It is the essence of all that is. It is one of the closest vibrations to God source we can attain in the physical realm." Jack

March 23 (My Birthday)

THE WAVES ARE CRASHING. I can't tell if the salt I taste is from the tears running down my cheeks or the salty air that surrounds me in a blanket of mist. My hair whips around my face as if it has a life force of its own, daring me to keep it tame. The rocks are sharp, dangerous, yet beckoning me forward as I cautiously navigate my way towards the edge where the land meets the ocean. A siren's song seems to wash over me. The waves are crashing around me and the spray of the ocean water leaves tiny, wet beadlets on my skin. The deafening sound of the waves breaking into a kaleidoscope of airborne color fills my ears and eyes with an intense energy that pales in comparison to the heartache that rips through my chest. I feel as if I'm in a dream, teetering on the edge of dimensional realities, being called to step into an altered state of awareness.

I stand on the brink of safety, looking out over the ocean as we had done so many times in this magically wild place. Momentarily, I look to my left and see you standing there on the rocky edge looking out over the ocean. The sight of you takes my breath away and reality becomes blurred. My heart races ahead of the ache already present. Then I realize it is a play of the dancing mist and light that has me fooled into thinking I saw you. And yet, I feel you next to me, breathing in sync with my breath. Perhaps you gifted me, my love, with the vision of you through a dissolved dimensional veil. Here we are together but I stand alone, a remaining sentinel to the couple we once were in physical form. I gaze out at the ocean again as my tears find freedom to flow amidst the sobs that take hold of my body. I find a strange comfort in the heart pain of my task ahead.

I scour the rocks, looking for the perfect spot to place your ashes so the waves will wash in and take you out to sea. Your dying wish; for me to take a trip and spread your ashes in the places you loved the most, this exact spot being your most treasured.

This stretch of beach held fond memories for both of us. The first year we were together, Jack saved all his money so he could bring me to this magical place, hoping I would find a soul connection to the land similar to his own. We crested a sand dune and walked towards the ocean, and I was mesmerized by the beauty before me. As we slowly strolled the beach, I was looking at all the irresistible rocks along the way. I came upon a stone with holes all over it buried in the sand. I was in love, not only with this man who made the trip possible but with nature's stunning creation positioned at my feet. He saw the same stone and, with care, started to uncover what turned out to be ocean-sculpted sandstone in the shape of a large oval obelisk. My eyes were beseeching as I looked at him and timidly asked if we could possibly take the enchanting stone home with us. His smile was as wide as I had seen and his eyes twinkled with child-like joy. He responded with "Of course we are taking this home. I was hoping you would feel it calling you too!"

It was like that with us, in complete resonance with each other. From our first meeting when we felt an immediate internal soul connection that seemed so familiar, until the day he uttered his last spoken words, "Oh my, I need to say goodbye to you now, Becki. I love you!" He then shakily leaned over to kiss me with his sweet lips one last, conscious time. We held each other and sobbed with the knowing that this part of our life together was finished. He then slipped into a restful coma before leaving his body completely. My earthly Jack showed me the sheer power of sacred love in that precious moment. Love that knows no bounds, that flies free from form and blends with the power of the universe.

That kind of love is possible. It is not just in fairytales that we can experience this type of divine love connection with another here. One key we felt brought us to rec-ognize this powerful relationship was we had both been doing our own inner soul work, healing the emotional wounds within us. By the time we met, we were ready to approach relationship from a place of wisdom, strength, and growth; not trauma or neediness.

But I have to say there was also an undeniable soul recognition, an awareness that we were destined to be together, that we had some aspect of life to experience beyond conscious insight. What we came together to accomplish was the very thing we have been conditioned to fear the most - death.

I don't mean we planned or knew the journey was going to end way too early or that it would end the way it did with Jack's terminal cancer diagnosis. What I do mean is that we had a higher mission to attain, one chosen by our souls before we came to Earth, one that would throw us into events I now share on these pages.

As I brush the tears from my eyes, I find it; the place I am going to put your ashes, my love. The rocks are jagged and the tide is coming in so I have to be extra careful with my balance. The last thing I need is to fall and be pulled out with the receding tumultuous waters. I focus on the small depression in the rocks that feels like the perfect place of honoring for you, Jack.

I brace myself and watch the rhythm of the waves as they crash onto shore. I have to get the timing just right because I will be washed out to sea if I falter. I put my hand in my coat pocket and feel the heart-shaped glass vase that houses your ashes along with rose petals, incense, and your guitar pick. I also have my phone.

I gaze out over the ocean and feel my heart pounding against my chest, my breath labored. I'm not sure I am ready but I feel you so strong next to me that I hit play on my phone's music file. You had asked me to please play a song for you (Dante's Prayer by Loreena McKennitt) when I honored your life. Now I find myself reminiscing about the many times I had seen you play this song and watched the tears stream down your cheeks because you were so moved. Now, the tears are all encompassing. The song plays underneath the booming of the wave explosions and I look out to sea and sing into the swirling wind through choking sobs.

Now, Becki, now.

I rush to the newly sacred spot and quickly pour your ashes out of the heart vessel. I feel you loving me, holding me, as I finish placing you into the glistening, wet rock depression. My eye is on the next wave rolling in. I have to hurry. There, my love. You are where you asked to be. My heart is racing in anticipation, unsure of how I will manage watching your ashes leave me.

I step back when the swell collides with the shore spraying white foam all over the jagged rock face. I watch your ashes as the waters make their way into the sacred depression. I am transfixed. Your ashes swirl around with the ocean waters and trickle out in a beautiful dance of energy in motion; I watch in utter bliss for you and complete heart-

break for me. Your ashes remain until the third wave finally washes them completely out to sea. I take a deep breath while watching the last of your physical presence leave. It is done. I cannot move; my body, mind, and soul feeling a part of this wonderfully wild environment, a part of me not wanting to say goodbye and yet I feel your love envelop me, reminding me you are absolutely by my side.

This beautiful beach will now carry a magic only we will know, my love, the magic of love everlasting.

We all experience our own form of letting go, of loss and the grief that inevitably follows. It matters not the nature of the loss, be it a loved one, a child, a pet, a job, financial security, friendship, divorce. The list is varied and vast. Yes, some losses impact us at a deeper and more profound soul level. So many of us experience the deep heart emotions stirred up due to the loss of someone or something. It is inescapable and part of our human experience.

One of the losses I am compelled to explore is the loss one feels with the death of a loved one. The words spilling out on this page are a testament to my beloved Jack, my soul mate, the man I knew I was destined to spend the rest of my life with. To lose the kind of love I shared with him threw my world into a tailspin I was not sure I would survive.

Like the ocean waves I watched break onto the shore as I spread his ashes, the waves of my emotional world had been turbulent, wild, and unpredictable since his transition.

On September 4, 2019, my beloved was diagnosed with terminal cancer. Twenty days later he was gone from my life. We performed conscious death together. It was a dive into a world neither of us had expected and yet we were pushed into accepting in ways beyond our comprehension.

After the first ten days, Jack knew it was not about his survival but about his passage into death of the physical. I was with him every step of the unpredictable path, devoted to his journey in the way only a beloved can understand and do. The kind of love it takes to step into the death passage with your soul mate cannot be described with words. I have tried. Words pale in comparison with the experience one must walk when loving into loss.

How did I do it? How did I find my way into the depths of the kind of love that helped me spend every moment at full attention to his death process, his needs, our love, and my letting go? How is it that I was able to write a book about conscious death and our miraculous afterlife connection? Why do I feel so compelled to write again, exposing my heart to the vulnerability of exploring life and love? Can I stand in my truth while I share with the world my journey?

These questions spurred me forward like a siren's song, the pull forward to a reality I was learning to discover and allow to unfold.

As I stood on the rocky shore looking out over the ocean, I knew the next writing was coming. I could hear Jack clearly reminding me we were not done. Life had so much more to bring to us, me on the planet and him in the divine. He had so much more he wanted to share with the world and I would be the vessel through which the words would flow.

My physical vessel, my body, was moving forward despite feeling stagnant at times and bobbing in the waters of new life without Jack. Sometimes movement only existed in each breath, each small action step that animated my body. It was extremely challenging to not fixate on the wake behind me, wanting the past to somehow create a different wave versus the one I was surfing, and yet the winds of change continued to blow, taking me, guiding me, pulling me towards a future I did not know how to embrace.

The questions in my soul continued to haunt me and I re-lived my beginnings with Jack. Our odyssey was a meeting of two souls destined to embrace the life we chose long before we met, a soul contract filled with higher purpose and meaning steeped in spiritual destiny.

It was instant recognition for him and a stirring deep in my subconscious but it was complicated. We were both still married, in relationships that had stopped working, were not of our highest expression, and we both knew it. Yet, we did our best to let the budding friendship be just that, a mutual respect and honoring of the circumstances we found ourselves in. We maintained friendship for four years.

But much like the force of the moon tides pulling the oceans' waters toward land with an unstoppable force, our connection was undeniable while both marriages were in collapse. We gave every chance for resolve within marriages that were choking the life force out of us. I prayed to GOD, please help me find the life I was supposed to be living. I know I am destined for something else.

And then it happened. Jack was done with his marriage while mine was still teetering on the edge of the cliff. The force behind our soul connection was growing stronger every day. In one of Jack's journals, I found his writing from that time.

"I can see your house from here, so far and yet so near. I'm torn between saving you and trusting in the source of all life. Time has seemed to almost stop within this space, I send divine love. I ask the "ONE" to be with you and to surround you with pure love. One must ask, Am I thinking life or am I feeling life? At times they are both present. How do I limit something that has no limits? Maybe it is too much for you, my love, and I should find a way to put a stop to how I feel. Yet, it feels so un-natural to stop what is my natural state of being - my source."

The energy exchange between us was palpable and magic existed at every turn. I was being guided by a hand that knew my destiny more than I but one I started to recognize as I embraced the tides of a divine soul love overtaking me.

Jack was a gifted musician, a guitar player, composer, and lover of the power of sound and its ability to move the human soul. I was pulled into his music in a way that defied words but dove into the realm of energy, an energetic exchange of power beyond the physical experience of hearing. He played his guitar every day and I was transported to places within my body and soul that were divine. At one point, he asked me to come and listen to a piece of music he had been working on. I sat down at his feet and watched as he began to strum. He was beauty in motion. I could feel the love pouring out of his hands, as if he was making love to the instrument. As I sat there and listened to the melody birthing into the air, I was immediately moved to tears. There was a deep stirring in me, a recognition of something beyond space and time into the domain of the sacred. I felt every note as they wound their way around my cells and vibrated to the core of my essence. When he finished, he gazed into my tear-filled eyes and told me it was my song; he had written it for me, it was how he felt about me in the form of song. He was secretly hoping I would recognize us, the union that was possible.

I will never forget the evening I saw Jack walking down our deserted country road, lost in the moment. I stepped into the street to watch what was taking place; he was about thirty feet in front of me, unaware I was there. The early evening light was setting and the sun's rays were casting the perfect silhouette on a newly hatched swarm of mayflies swirling around and engulfing him in a dance of movement that was ethereal. He was moving his hands in slow motion in response to the whirling insects enveloping him and the waves of flow that occurred were like watching water move around his body effortlessly. I observed this scene for several minutes, taken in by the sheer beauty of the dance between this man and nature. I then walked into the swarm to join him and, for a few moments, I felt the absolute rapture of nature's joy caressing us. The love I felt was vibrating in every cell of my body.

One day I was sharing that I felt like I was at the edge of a cliff and my choice was to either stay frozen in my existing life or to free fall into the unknown. Jack peered into my eyes and said, "I have already jumped, my love, and I am flying. I am here if you care to fly with me. Take my hand." Again, the hand of love was reaching out to me. What was I going to choose?

Then it happened, the defining moment when I took his hand towards our inevitable contract, the fulfilling of a design we intuitively knew and yet had no idea truly how it would evolve. I will never forget the day.

One hot summer afternoon, Jack was helping me move some items from one business location to another. Due to the heat, a floor fan was running to keep air flowing. I had music playing loudly in the background and was busy putting items away on a shelf. All of a sudden, I felt the energy in the room shift. I turned around to see what had changed my awareness. Jack was gazing intensely at the fan. A feather someone had tied to the outside rim of the fan was blowing in the breeze. Then, I noticed what had him so mesmerized. I, too, gazed in amazement at the feather dancing in the fan's wind, realizing its dance was perfectly synchronized with the music playing in the background. Reality shifted into a syncing of consciousnesses, awareness of becoming one combined energy as we both watched the magic taking place before our eyes and ears. I was as much in awe of Jack as I was the feather in the fan. He regularly saw magic in the smallest of life's details, and because of that, I, too, was blessed to participate in those moments.

Later in the afternoon Jack helped me move games. Our love was blossoming and the intensity of the moments were growing hard to ignore. Somewhere in the heat of the afternoon we found our first kiss. It was exciting, full of possibility. We had the discussion of how this would change our lives, which were complicated, not free and easy. It was a difficult task to think of possibilities and yet that was exactly where we found ourselves. A love so strong, so natural, there was no holding back the deep waters behind the dam.

As we were driving home, he said to me, "Imagine the possibilities. Imagine what our lives could be together. Imagine the amazing love we could share. Just imagine, Becki."

Later that night as I was getting ready for bed, I felt something in my shoe. I took it off and shook out the small object. To my utter shock and blissful surprise, it was a small magnet from a word game that said IMAGINE. Somehow, as I was moving games that day, the one-word magnet fell into my shoe while I had them off, under the table. Chills ran through my entire body and I knew divine intervention had taken place. I felt blessed by Spirit and ecstatic that my love would no longer be denied.

Spirit moving physical matter was not new to me. Several times in my life, unexplainable events took place and physical manifestation of a divinely guided message spoke to me. I was blessed by a reading in which my guide spoke through the person channeling to honor me for paying attention to change in my surroundings. He wanted me to know that I often had physical items move and to keep noticing those small details. It was Spirit's way of getting my attention.

I could not wait to show Jack so I ran down the street and knocked on his door. When he answered, I breathlessly handed him the magnet. I said, "Here, this is yours. Spirit sent me the message loud and clear and now this is yours. I am ready to take your hand. I am ready to fly!"

The magnet was always with Jack in the years that followed. He placed it on his most prized possession, his guitar headstock, a reminder of the day everything changed. His guitar was used in the most precious gift I was ever given. It was Valentine's Day and I stepped into my car to go to work. Poking out of the car CD player was a disk labeled Happy Valentine's Day, My Love. The pink sticky note attached said, "Play Me."

As I drove to work that day, I played the disk with his hand written words. Jack had recorded a heartfelt message over music he had composed for me, showcasing his devotion of our love connection.

Jack's Valentine's Day Message to Becki

Hello, My Love. I'm sure this is coming as a surprise to you. Happy Valentine's Day. I just wanted to put something together to let you know how much I love you and how much you really mean to me. This is a day when everyone celebrates their affection for someone else. There really are no words to describe how much you mean to me. You have been the greatest gift that has come into my life. I am lit up inside in ways I never have been because of your presence. You've made a huge difference in my life and hopefully I have made some difference in your life as well. I think we share that. There's going to be a lot of people who are going to get candy and exotic gifts on this day but there won't be any of that coming your direction. I think you know why. So you're getting it in this form. I have never done this before and it is kind of odd hearing my voice, because the other night we were doing this with you. I just want to say that I love you more than anything on this planet. You mean everything to me and I am grateful you are in my life. I look forward to what our future holds. I think it is all good and it is only going to get better. It is quite a journey doing it with you and I wouldn't have it any other way. I'm not always eloquent or have the right words or I come out a little brash. I mean well but I don't always get it put into the right words to have the arrow hit its mark. And so in lieu of that, I am just going to say that this is the day you get to rejoice in that someone loves you madly. You are special and you are always going to be special. You can love yourself and honor yourself because you are this incredible bright light. I will leave you with this because I could ramble on. You know I don't have any problem talking. Not sure where you are right now. You might be close to the center of town, I'm not sure. But in any event, this is to uplift you so I will leave you with a piece of my heart. You might want to pull over and listen to track two. I don't want you getting teary eyed driving because I know how easily you can cry sometimes. Maybe you won't and that might be a good thing. Nevertheless, I leave you with this. I love you dearly.

When his loving words stopped, the music he composed for me continued to play. While the car was pulled off the road, he was uplifting my soul, infusing me with his soul essence. And he was right, the tears flowed as I absorbed the message and the music filling me with the love of this man I adored. Work could wait.

I still have the magnet and it continues to inspire me to imagine our life together, only now it is a life with me here on the planet and him in the afterlife. Who knew that twelve years later I would be writing a bestselling book titled, "20 Days Changed Everything - A Love Story Moving Through Conscious Death to Afterlife Connection". The day he transitioned into his afterlife, I took a vow to always imagine the possibilities.

Breathing in the smell of air flowing off the surface of the ocean, I continue to gaze over the rolling waves into the vast distance. I am feeling resolve. My love for you, Jack, will remain a part of my eternal soul but I am ready to move forward. I am honored that I have been blessed to continue our relationship in this new way, full of a divine and sacred love connection. I will always cherish this rocky shoreline, the place where our love expressed itself so freely.

In your honor, Jack, I plan to walk the beach looking for any treasure you and Gaia, the living Earth, choose to share with me. I take one last breath into the waves of my internal ocean, one last look from this rocky point, knowing full well this will be the last time I ever visit this place. My journey is now a walk into something new.

Back in the hotel room that night, I checked in with Jack. It had been nearly a year and a half since Jack passed and channel writing with him in his afterlife soul expression became an activity we shared often. The writing is not my own but a combined energy of oneness for the journey taken, the contract fulfilled. The sunset of our physical relationship was but a part of a larger plan; that of helping others become aware of life after death, communication beyond the veil, and the sacred love that knows no bounds existing in this physical world.

How did I navigate all of the questions? I asked myself. I navigated my life through a reckoning with my own paradigms of belief, digging deep within my soul to discover the switch, the switch that flips on the light of awareness to the beauty of life, here in the physical and the eternal. I found my strength through a willingness to feel all the emotions that came up, to not judge myself, to be open and vulnerable to my heart, my sharing, but mostly, to remember LOVE. I walked through all I experienced through my continuing love story with Jack and a Christ Conscious love that was connected to a power greater than myself, GOD.

Jack's Message

Given to Becki February 17, 2021

It is a beautiful service we offer now, my love, part of the amazing journey we chose. You have the ability to hold others in compassion and this is part of our plan, our contract together. I will keep encouraging you, holding you up as you navigate your third dimensional experience while you move into even higher dimensions of reality. I am connecting with so many now, the release of our first book has people asking, wondering, talking to me and I am so happy to be sharing an energy exchange of this love vibration. People are feeling into their loved ones and the angels are singing, helping us with connections to those who are ready. This book is needed in the world.

I love and honor you, Becki.

Chapter 2

THE RISING TIDE

April 2021

*"The power of sacred and divine love radiates
out into the world and impacts others, ignites
that flame within others."* Jack

A MIDST THE SHEER PAIN of letting go of Jack, I found myself hopeful for a future. I was finally feeling like I was ready to live again. I had stood on the rocky shores spreading his ashes on my birthday one and a half years after his passage. I had months during that time not sure I would survive the extreme heartache that engulfed my every cell and yet at other moments experiencing the magic and awe of our afterlife connection. I so desperately wanted to find my way to a life beyond pain and I was feeling the pull of Spirit within me to keep going. I had an internal knowing that I was not done with life and yet I questioned being here without him present.

I was surprised when the spark of desire for a new relationship came into my field. Not sure I was ready and yet giving me a glimmer of hope there might be a future beyond my loss. I never dreamed it would be possible but a higher awareness kept nudging me to remember the journey, a meandering path to love in its many forms. It was as if Jack was telling me, "Don't forget who you are, my love. You are a heart-based soul on the planet. Continue to spread love and light. Honor who you are. I want you to go forward in the love of another."

The messages I and others had received from Jack were clear; his love for me would never die; it was eternal but he wanted me to find happiness while on Earth. He wanted me to find another love, another man to enjoy my life with. It felt like the highest form of love, divine, unconditional, compassionate, the type of love we shared with each other while together in physical form. Thus, I knew his messages to be true.

I began to find comfort in the idea of not being alone for the rest of my life. I am such a loving soul that feeling I was going to spend my life alone made it almost impossible to see a happy future. Being a sensual person, touch is a part of my solace, part of my divine feminine expression. Making love with Jack was a sacred act. We honored each other, our bodies, and our souls with a breathless beauty and timeless oneness beyond anything I had ever experienced before. I was blessed in that Jack radiated a divine masculine counter to my divine feminine. I did not want to imagine the possibility of never experiencing that in my life again.

God gifted me with the awareness of possibility, the intersection of past, present, and future love in a way I could neither doubt nor deny. What would it be like to have

Jack in my life from his realm while holding another in the physical? Was that too strange? I found myself headed into uncharted waters.

And then it happened.

Despite feeling the glimmer of brighter future while traveling to the places I spread Jack's ashes, I dove into the depths of despair. How was it possible to have such an incredible connection to him only to find myself in the darkest place yet? I mean, I had written a best-selling book about our love and my nine-month journey after his transition. How could I fall now, just when life seemed ready to expand, to go forward, to find new meaning? I seemed to be losing myself. It felt as if I was spiraling into the abyss of darkness through a whirlpool of my own grief.

My dear friend Adele was with me on the journey as we spread Jack's ashes. I could not have faced the travel by myself and she held me while I cried and poured out my sorrows. She was a life raft in the tumultuous waters I was sailing. At moments, it felt like she was the only thing keeping me from drowning in my own tears, her love of me and Jack the stability needed to navigate the storm.

With her by my side, I was able to breathe into my moments, taking one step, and then one more step, and then one more step, until we arrived home. I was depleted. I was questioning everything in my reality, all the while feeling a small inkling of awareness to the bigger picture. Why me? *Why did I have to be the one at life's helm, Jack?* I desperately needed support and I knew the love of family and friends was mandatory or I would be engulfed by the tides of my emotions rising higher than the shores of my psyche could handle, drowning me under the waves of grief.

A couple months earlier, though a mutual friend, I had met a woman who was to play a key role in my healing journey. Her name is Barbara and she came to my rescue with an offer of a safe haven and energy healing for my wounded soul. She is a powerful energy healer who became a soul sister in short order. We found a kinship in each other that stretched beyond time and space. Our lives, our work, our passions, our love, our connection to God, Jesus, Mother Mary, Mary Magdalene, were all on a similar track. When she offered her home and her expertise, I jumped at the chance to be with her. God was guiding both of us to this destined meeting.

The timing for a visit to see her was perfect. I had planned a trip with my brother to go see our mom in Arizona and I was able to arrange to see Barbara right before that trip. Again, God played a hand in helping guide me along to the next indicated action and Jack was right there as my support; I felt his love in my heart and body in a deeply visceral way.

I arrived at Barbara's home on April 6. We fell into each other's arms as long-lost sisters welcoming each other home. We automatically dove into energy healing work and did a meditation that night, bringing us both to tears of joy and empowerment. Jack's energy was clearly present and Barbara is a gifted channel and medium so communication flowed effortlessly. The unfolding of events would take us both on a journey into so much more than we knew, a part of the collective energy of evolution and ascension.

The next day, Barbara and I had a BQHT (Beyond Quantum Healing Hypnosis) session. Again, Jack was present immediately and communicated with us both. We asked Jack if there was anything he would like to share about the session we had the night before.

He told us we were surrounded by so many souls, indicating we were learning to hold the energy of higher frequency. He said we were coming together, so honored and loved, in the understanding of who we are as divine feminine women. We experienced a small piece of the energy of our potential. We were learning how to hold the frequencies and the healings that are available to us humans.

As Barbara led me into the BQHT session, I saw the color purple, was completely surrounded by the color purple, infiltrated by the color purple. It provided a cocoon of safety for me and it felt comforting as I dove deeper into healing, becoming one with the sacred purple light, the frequency of that light, allowing the light to become one with me. The light merged into me through my crown chakra and then through my energy centers. The purple light surrounded every cell, every molecule, clearing and cleansing my body through its movement.

At some point, my body went into a complete state of quantum hypnosis. Jack came through to me and he helped me remember who I was. He reminded me that I embody compassion for others; that I am light, divine love energy. The following words are the channeled message that came through me as I was under hypnosis, the flow of language staggered, a complexity to the underlying multidimensional message that was imparted.

We (Jack and I) showed up together in form as an honoring of, and a merging of, all expressions of the vibration of love. The divine feminine is what I, as Becki, am here to share. He is asking me to love myself first and foremost, to see myself as he sees me. He asks me to write, saying, "the gift is in the writing, and the growth, and the forgiveness. The book to come is a gift in sharing and teaching others. The grief and pain felt will then be transmuted to the other side of divine light and love."

The work we do together in vibration is us, who we are. The work I do with people as Becki, opens an energy portal and he is there helping me. We are a team. He is telling me to trust that.

(The channeling then transitioned from Jack's energy to an energy akin to the Divine Goddess Mother coming through the human Becki). We (humans) are learning how to Embody higher frequencies. The physical body is adjusting. As we learn to hold the higher frequencies, our body learns to adapt. We are holding power...and in that power, transmutation happens naturally.

We (humans) are sharing that, teaching that, stepping into the light, with so much power at our disposal. We are learning how to hold these higher frequencies in the body. As we hold the frequencies, we are helping Gaia. That is why Gaia is coming in so strong. (I was feeling the energy of the living Earth very dynamic in my awareness along with Mary Magdalene) Gaia is holding us in this time of ascension. Mary Magdalene's presence and the rise of the Divine feminine is a balancing of it all.

We, as divine feminine humans, understand pain, grief, heartache, physical hardships, and yet we are able to hold it with so much light, through so much light - the doorway of so much light, the light of awareness. We can't understand these deep awarenesses without going through them; to understand we must go through the doorway. (Note: the doorway symbolized all the pain and suffering held in the divine light of love). Walking through the doorway is the transmutation, transformation, and alchemization that the energy, (the light, vibration and frequency) is seeking.

(At this point, my body began to physically respond as if it was channeling the energy of the whole of the divine feminine, not separate from the collective consciousness but reacting as if my body was a singular conduit for all women. I was feeling intense constriction in my lower abdomen followed by an energy release of expansion and lightness. The words that follow came from a collective divine feminine, many voices through my one form.)

The sacral chakra is being infused with density, a holding of the energy for eons, the heartache of the divine feminine. We have to transmute through the feminine, through the human physicality, to hold healing for the body. It is almost overwhelming. I'm being encouraged to hold it; eons and eons of heartache. The healing that needs to take place is massive! Allow. Allow. Allow a holding of the vibration of that density in the body.

It is safe. Mary Magdalene is holding our hands. She is holding the light. We (women) are the conduit that has to be. We have to be. We hold the physical feminine principle. We have to be able to bring in through the physical body, the alchemy of the pain. The density felt in the body is so old, and yet there is no time. It's the Sophia Goddess Energy calling to us, the Divine feminine energies that are so ancient and yet rising on the planet.

So, it is time to show the way, show the way, show the way. To stand in the light through the pain, through the shame, through the guilt of eons. To stand in the light with all expressions of the wounding of the divine.

The Divine masculine collective wants healing. That is Jack's role. That's the piece he holds, the healing he wants as well. The alchemization of both (divine feminine and divine masculine) is where we are headed. The ascension of our reality, a new Earth, is a healing of this balance.

We, as Divine feminine, are holding, transmuting, and al-chemizing; feeling the constrictions in our sacral chakra as light then moves in to then expand and release. We are *holding the waves in the body; absorption of the energies and vibrations of density and expansion.*

We are feeling density in the solar plexus and the sacral chakra, constriction, there for so long. The power we hold as the Divine feminine has been hidden, shamed, shut down, challenged, guilted. We are feeling the magnitude of all the shame being held and hidden, the heartache, the deep, dark density of it all.

It is time to allow light to be moved into awareness, shed light to be shown on our pain, on our shame, on the abuse, on the holding back we have done to ourselves, the hiding we have done for eons, the things we didn't do, the shaming of ourselves, because we didn't feel safe, we couldn't share, we were hurt, or we were killed. So much suffering of who we were and the power we held, so we kept it quiet. We let people think we were less than; we didn't shine our light so we would be protected. Those of us who are here now have the ability to feel all the pain, suffering, grief, heartache, shame, guilt; the power to hold it, to shift it, to alchemize it, as we ascend, share light and bring in the power of the divine feminine in complete balance with the divine masculine.

The Becki here is not separate from any other woman doing this work. We are here transforming all the suffering through our physical body's own pain and suffering. We have the ability. We are doing it for all, for our ancestry, the Divine feminine, and Gaia, so we can move into the new world

We (humans) hold the power, hold the power, hold the power. We are meant to be. It is the death of old ways. We hold death in the palm of our hands as we step into a new light. The old (death) is just the birthing of a new expression.

This is the energy Jack and I hold, the new energy through grief and pain, the stepping into a power of energy through the threshold of death into new birth, a new life. There are those humans here that hold this energy awareness, understand the memories, and then alchemize to shift it. Because we hold it all. We hold it all.

At this point in the session Barbara thanked all of the guides and the awarenesses that had come through. They said......

"Thank you for being on the planet; so many souls are doing the work of ascension. It has to happen through your physical bodies. We are so honored. We don't see you as less than us, we see you as so much more."

No words could describe the blessed, divine energy we were enveloped in, when Jack came through and said, "This is what I see. This is how I see you. I am forever holding you."

The awareness of healing beyond what I imagined became evident and the feeling of gratitude permeated my soul. It was the perfect segue into a class I had been planning called Dancing the Divine Feminine, the calling within my soul to move into an aspect of myself while supporting other women to explore their divine feminine essence.

I was buzzing from the high energy frequencies my body had experienced and the energy in me remained hopeful, full of the love of Jack, Spirit, and God. The ability we have as humans to step into elevated states, higher frequencies, vibrations or quickening, is an aspect of expansion we all have access to. How we reach those states varies among people but meditation, energy healing work, nature, love, faith, God, all can bring the soul and body into closer resonance within. It can be felt at a cellular level, often in the form of tingles up the spine, an elevation of mood, or an all-encompassing calm and peace that fills the body, mind, and soul completely.

I arrived at my mom's home on April 8th in preparation for traveling with my brother to Arizona to pick her up and bring her back home to Idaho for the summer. The house was empty, I was alone in complete silence. The stage was set for another energy experience of divine connection.

As I write this story of a year in my life, I realize the human condition can be a delicate balance of vulnerability and exposure. I wrestled with the idea of sharing, in a very public way, the event that took place that evening. While tapping into my higher awareness and Jack, I felt drawn to be authentically real and speak my truth in a way that helps me move beyond my fear of being judged by others, to recognize the value in allowing the story of my healing to be fully told.

Moving into physical states of higher frequency was a practice I continued to learn and integrate within myself; as an energy sensitive person, I became adept at sensing the subtle shifts in energy within my body. I was learning to work with my body and spirit through the beautiful dance of energy movement and my sacred love with Jack remained a strong element in my exploration. In my first book, I alluded to the potential to remain deeply connected in undying love between two souls, a mystical union that knows not the bounds of space and time. The love we experienced was beyond mere romance and lust but an authentic pattern within each of us forged in a strong erotic connection, spiritual yearning, and innate emotional trust. This form of love is mentioned in the Bible's Song of Solomon as the "Lover and the Beloved". The erotic, sexual energy present between two souls, strong enough to forge a fusion that holds the two formerly separate individualities into a bonding of one soul, the "Abler Soul".

That night, alone in the silence of my room, I conversed with Jack. My body began to vibrate and my energy rose. I was used to feeling Jack near me, the subtle shift in my aura, the energy field around my body changing to a cool sensation and my skin tingling with his touch. I began to feel his cool etheric body enter mine and as our energies merged, I experienced a form of lovemaking never talked about. The possibility of an orgasmic experience with your beloved from the afterlife had never been in my realm of possibility and yet, here I was in a form of divine ecstasy only known to those who fully surrender to this type of bond.

Was I crazy? Perhaps. Was it possible to move into relationship in this way beyond the veil? Yes! While my courage grew in delicately sharing this experience as I walked this version of love with Jack, I came to understand I was not alone in this type of afterlife lovemaking. I met many others along the way who claimed they had experienced it too. This form of divine lovemaking crosses all ages, timelines, and demographics; the only thing present in all those I encountered was a deep and abiding love with their beloved on the other side of the veil. It mattered not whether the person believed in afterlife connection; it happened often spontaneously yet very physically to those I spoke with.

The gift of our divine love was healing me and, unbeknownst to me, that dive into the depths of love and healing was only the surface ripple of what I was going to need to survive as I headed into a life-altering event.

Eleven days later on April 19, I found the lump in my left breast. As I stood in the shower that night, the water droplets raining down on my body, I had a sinking feeling I was headed into choppy waters. The sudden weight loss now seemed ominous yet was the very catalyst for the lump being found. Life was pulling me to breathe into the deep water of love, all versions of love. Jack's message carried a depth I would need yet not fully understand. What was in store for me?

Jack's Message

April 24

I am here, my love. The subtle shift in your energy field is the blending of our souls, the balancing of a journey we have taken so many times. It is nice you are writing, my love. Writing is one key to continued connection. You are never alone. I have become part of your essence. Trust in that depth of love.

Chapter 3

THE RISING WAVES CRASH

May 2021

*"In this now moment, all is perfect, well; you
are on track with your journey. Rest into that
awareness. Stay strong, my love."* Jack

LIFE ROLLED ALONG AND my work continued uninterrupted. I did my best to ride the waves that seemed to build in tandem as my body felt more ill at ease but I also knew I did not want to dive into fear of the unknown. I trusted my journey as much as one can when facing uncharted waters, trying to find an elusive compass.

Fortunately, I had a Usui/Holy Fire III® Reiki Level I and II class scheduled the first weekend of May. I am a Usui/Holy Fire III® Reiki Master/Teacher/Practitioner. I will be the first to tell anyone I meet about the wonderful healing properties of Reiki energy. Being immersed in a training for a whole weekend was exactly what my soul needed. I teach these classes with two amazing women, Diana and Inge, who are masters in their own right and, when the three of us come together to teach, magic happens.

One of the practices that assisted me in moving grief through my body was meditation. I am blessed to be a highly visual intuitive when it comes to guided meditation journeys. I was excited to support my walk into the unknown with my physical body by adding a dose of food for my soul. When I relax and allow myself to go into mediation, Jack can easily reach me from his realm of existence. In the world of Usui/Holy Fire III® Reiki Training, meditation is a prominent feature. So, it was a regular occurrence that Jack joined me in many of the experiences and this training was to be no different.

I knew the timing was perfect. My body and soul needed comfort.

May 1, 2021

Journal Entry for Reiki Level I & II

Ocean of Holy Love Meditation

Going into the meditation, I was a little disjointed due to some technical issues at the beginning of the class. Yet, as I found myself walking down the path through the enchanting forest, the familiar redwood forest, I felt the hint of Jack ahead of me. I walked to the ocean and before my eyes I saw a stunning sunset. There were colors of red, orange, pink, and gold rippling across the water's surface. Jack walked towards me from the light I was gazing into. He was positioned between Jesus and Mary Magdalene as they all walked towards me. Jack reminded me it is all okay, my life is going to be okay. I felt a sense of peace wash over my body, filling my body, my heart, my soul. Jack said to me, "In this now moment, all is perfect, well; you are on track with your journey. Rest into that awareness. Stay strong, my love."

When I came out of the meditation, I felt a sense of peace that set the tone for the rest of the weekend's training. I was ready for whatever Spirit, God, and Jack had to show me.

Reiki Placement Meditation

Jack and I walked but my awareness was quite spotty at first. I had a hard time seeing him though I did sense him. I felt someone else at the top of the hill lying next to me and was a little confused about why this person was there because in that moment, I only wanted Jack. Then I realized Jack was there too and I softened into the connection with all three of us. All of a sudden, it was just me in this place where there had been three and my guides took me on a journey, showing me information. I felt one of the students, and was given information to help him with a challenge he was facing. My guides then told me to show him a certain picture I had and to share with him what I knew about his burdens. They showed me other people who were carrying burdens and informed me I hold keys that will help them, if I am ready, if I choose to step fully in, to let go of my own fears, my own shames, my own hesitations. I was then surrounded with peace and love. I fell into a complete state of calm within.

One of the awarenesses I have is an understanding of the power of meditation and energy healing work. We are not only physical humans; we are energetic beings, first and foremost, who have the ability to tap into the unlimited potential within us to heal, to create miracles in our lives, to move beyond our perceived limitations to strengths we did not know existed. I called on this internal strength even as my body continued to feel strange, not my normal vibrant self.

On the second day of our class, the meditations seemed even more powerful than the first and I allowed my awareness to open more while continuing to develop my trust meter.

May 2, 2021

Journal Entry for Reiki Level I & II

Holy River Meditation

I was with Jack. The forest I was in was the familiar Redwoods. It was magical. We played hide-and-seek around a big tree, breathed in the damp, earthy smells, and looked at some small mushrooms. We laughed and it was playful as we walked to this huge river. We followed the river upstream until it became smaller and we approached the river's bend. We stopped to admire the shimmering of diamond-like sparkles on the waters surface. He gently took my hands and guided me to a waterfall. He asked me to step inside with him. The water fell over my body and I was aware it was Divine, coming directly from the heavens. Jack stepped back and women gathered around me, surrounding me, bathing me, holding me, encouraging me to let the density in my body wash away. They pulled out trauma, grief, sadness, and pain. Not just from this life but from many lives. I allowed the waterfall to wash over me as they worked on me. Then Jack re-entered the waterfall. He joined me and said the marriage of the Divine Masculine and the Divine Feminine was what we share. Our path was right on track. "NO REGRETS!" he said to me. It is a balancing of the Divine aspects of us, within relationship with all: partnerships, family, friends, and self. Then I allowed the healing waters to just flow. Funny that the movie The Matrix popped into my head. I wondered why but then smiled at the mysterious nature of our so-called reality.

I asked family and friends to support me, to hold a strong vision of healing while I set up the necessary doctors' appointments to explore the lump so prominent in my left breast. I connected with Jack, my guides, and God, praying for strength to stay in peace with what my body showed me.

May 18

Barbara had a conversation with Jack who had information to share with me.

The lump is a "pocket of un-wellness." Jack says it would heal on its own, but of course you can't ignore it now that you know of its existence. The more attention placed on it actually inflames the condition, emotional attention and physical attention. There is no purpose to this exercise of awareness except maybe to be in more of a place of trust; trust in your journey, trust in your path, trust in your movement through all situations, conditions, and information. Do you have this much trust? You are developing super powers in trust.

Jack says, "Try not to overthink your pretty head about this. It wastes effort and energy."

Once again, I was encouraged to trust in my journey. This can be a gargantuan task for the human mind that wants to feel safe, secure, wants the outcome to be known. Uncertainty within the body can trigger one of humanity's greatest fears: physical suffering and death. I began to question what was in store for me and the words "breast cancer" popped into my mind during moments of silent contemplation. How could it not?

As my month progressed, I sought the counsel of a woman who channels beings of light who introduce themselves to her as The Light Keepers. Jack, being the ever-present spiritual warrior and guide for me that he is, made himself known right away. He encouraged me to let go of fear, reminding me I had it in me to heal, this experience was on track for my growth. The Light Keepers offered advice for physical healing that included certain foods, more water, releasing limiting belief patterns and emphasizing higher vibrational thought patterns and ways of viewing my life. Was I ready to listen? I thought so, but the deep-seated and unconscious part of me was yet to reveal itself.

Tapping into my inner knowing, I knew I needed to accept energy healing from others. I was keenly aware that my body wanted to voice what was going on so I had a Reiki session with friend and colleague, Diana. We both knew Reiki healing would guide us into an energy field of discovery.

As we started the session, a tremendous amount of energy release began happening on the left side of my body, and through the left breast. The release was in waves of chills, tingles, intense breathing, and subtle body movement. The Divine Feminine aspect of us resides mostly on the left side of the body while the Divine Masculine is represented on our right. The Divine Feminine reminds us to nurture ourselves, to see into the dark recesses of our psyche, to embrace the intuitive nature of who we are and allow our creative juices to flow. The Divine Masculine shows us how to forge ahead and make our dreams a reality in form, the protective and active side of our nature. But again, we are complex energetic beings and it is a balancing of all aspects within us that matters. What I did know: the more my body could step into a higher frequency vibration, the more healing ability my body could tap into.

My body was falling into alignment with the BQHT session I had done with Barbara in April. While lying on the table, my breast began to speak to me through my heart and mind. My breast said, "We miss our uterus. We miss our uterus." I was taken by surprise at those words. I had had surgery in 2011 to remove several large fibroid cysts and the uterus due to bleeding and pain complications. My ovaries remained. It was very clear to me that my breast tissue was speaking about the loss of my uterus. During the rest of the session, we offered loving energy healing to my breast tissue that was in grief, grief of losing not only my uterus but the huge loss of Jack in my life, the man who had nurtured and held me in this realm when I could not hold and nurture myself. I honored the tears flowing while my body received.

At my doctor's appointment, she immediately referred me for a mammogram. I was to see the x-ray technicians before month's end. I also took action to jump head first into working with my friend and Health Coach, Sharon. I was determined to give my body the best possible opportunity for healing I could access. I know the amazing potential that exists within each of us to move mountains with our health and wellbeing. I have seen seemingly miraculous spontaneous healing. It is an absolute reality if you choose to believe. Due to everything that had happened in my life after Jack transitioned with Spirit and the opening up of spiritual channels, I learned to be receptive to all possibilities. Despite the outcome with Jack's cancer journey, I knew my body could create miracles if that was my chosen path. Besides, I still held the vision of the lump being benign.

May 25

This morning as I am getting ready to go get the biopsy, I feel the pull to draw another piece of paper from the Gratitude Jar Jack and I used to add pieces of paper on which our gratitudes were written. I haven't touched it since last New Year's Day when I pulled Jack's note that I wrote a story about in the book The Grateful Soul. I let Spirit guide my hand and this is what I pulled!

"I'm grateful for Life! And all the beautiful forms it takes. Thank you for Becki and her love for me." Jack

An affirmation of LIFE and his gratitude for my love. Wow! I needed him today to remind me it is all okay. The breast lump feels smaller and continues to shrink in size so perhaps he is right. It will heal on its own.

In fact, I have wondered if I should even go get the biopsy but I am stepping into trust that it will be just fine, regardless of how circumstances show themselves. Some part of me knew I need to medically and energetically address what the lump was showing me and my body.

The mammogram was clear; a mass of tissue was present that was of grave concern. I stayed for an ultrasound and a biopsy was highly recommended. I agreed to have the tissue checked. The tumor in the left breast was 2.2 centimeters in size, alerting my medical team of the possible road ahead.

I found myself staying in the field of healing potential. I connected with Jack constantly and reminded myself to trust. I was drinking water infused with the word trust on the glass, based on the research of Dr. Masaru Emoto's water experiments. I prayed to find strength for whatever the outcome.

On May 27, I traveled with my daughter, son-in-law, and grandchildren to my mother's home for Memorial Day weekend. We had been in the car a mere five minutes when I got a call from my doctor. She informed me the tumor was Invasive Ductile Carcinoma, Stage 3 Breast Cancer. Just over 20 months after Jack passed, I heard the word Cancer again only this time it was not Jack and his lungs, it was me and my breast. The wave was crashing onto the shores of my paradigm. I heard Jack repeating to me, "TRUST Becki, TRUST!"

We humans have the capacity to feel many emotions, the heart center offering up a multitude of expressions for us to experience as we navigate our humanity. The feeling of shock can send waves of instant heat and sharp needles throughout the body. The news given by my doctor was no exception. It was what I felt when I heard the news about Jack as we sat in the ER that fateful evening. My shock then turned into a numb sensation as I absorbed what this meant in my current reality. I would be facing some tough decisions.

Life often presents us with choice points that impact our existence and shift us onto another life path trajectory. Was I committed to staying on the planet? Was I ready to move forward with a life without Jack's physical presence? Was I ready to walk with life and not death, change the outcome from 20 months earlier?

I continued to seek answers through my own internal pondering and writing as well as through the guidance of skillful energy practitioners.

May 31

Barbara Reading from an Oracle Card Deck (Gaia Oracle by Toni Carmine Salerno)

I just did a three card pull, past, present, future for you and, oh my gosh, they feel so amazingly accurate. This is so beautifully perfect as it comes through! Trust that you are being supported and guided, for sure! I get to trust this as well! It feels like something there is no escaping, because it is so challengingly perfect. Damn it.

"Past Card – Purification (Fire) – What is it that your heart truly desires? What do you perceive is missing in your life? In order to find the answers, you must look inside your heart. You already know this but have been reluctant to look because a part of you fears what your heart is trying to tell you. The only way forward is to face your fear. Something in your life is not working out as you would have liked and it's not going to get any better unless you have the courage to face it."

"Present Card – Perception – The lady on this card looks directly at the observer. She radiates love and wisdom, yet stands firmly in her own truth. From this standpoint she is

able to see beyond the veil of illusion. She has shown up in your reading today to reflect these same qualities within you. You are advised to stand your ground with regards to a particular person or issue. Stand within your own truth and don't be swayed by another's beliefs, opinions, or views. If it doesn't feel right, then it's not; trust your intuition and gut feeling on this one. Be true to yourself. You can respect another's views without having to change your value systems. If it doesn't align with your values, then don't take it on."

"Future Card – Gaia – The Gaia card is the most powerful card in this deck. It shows that you have a deep spiritual connection to Earth and a deep spiritual understanding of life. Gaia, the Earth Mother, thanks you for the love and consideration you show towards her and the love you have for all living things. She encourages you to gently and lovingly share your wisdom and knowledge of Earth with others. You are a beacon of light – remain that way. Share your knowledge and wisdom only with those who are ready to hear it and do not fear the Earth changes that are taking place, for all is evolving and unfolding as it should. All the Earth needs is a little more love."

Jack constantly reminded me it was not my time, that I still had other things left to do on the Earth plane. I also felt the hand of God, Jesus, Mother Mary, and Mary Magdalene supporting me as I sought help from family, friends, and professionals to move me through another layer of grief, my heart feeling appreciation for the insights I was learning. And yet........

Could I use my powerful knowing and align with energy healers who could help me heal? Was it possible that transmuting the breast through cancer to health was part of the pain and suffering I was alchemizing, not only for myself, but for the Divine Feminine, alchemizing the DEEPEST recesses of pain being released for so many in the collective feminine consciousness?

Jack's Message

May message to Becki

I am here, my love. The subtle shift in your energy field is the blending of our souls, a balancing of a journey we have taken so many times. It is good you are writing, my love. Writing is a key to continued connection. The energy rises may not seem as strong but there will be times when you feel me as strongly as you did at your moms. You are never alone and I support you when I can but you are finding your way. You will learn to move beyond me and not need me as much, even though I know you do not want to hear that. It is truth. I have become part of your essence, my love, and you are here to shine bright in your own right. Trust in that depth of love.

Chapter 4

UNCHARTED WATERS

June 2021

"Allow your tears to be the elixir that quenches the thirst of others who know the grief frequency, who need to be seen, heard, and honored. It is not about healing the grief, it is about loving it, embracing it, allowing it voice, giving to the energy of it. You can do it. Hold all the energies of the heart, my love, as it reverberates into the cosmos." Jack

HOW COULD I BEGIN to hold the power of life and vitality through so much nausea? Since I heard the word cancer, again, my body reacted with an energetic hit of shock and trauma washing over me like a tsunami engulfing me and drowning my appetite for food. I felt as if I was in a whirlpool going round and round the cancer vortex with my partner who was living in a different dimensional reality. I wasn't sure which way to point my broken compass while the energy of the vortex tried to pull me into despair. After all, cancer was how my beloved Jack left this realm. My experience from 20 months earlier was the emotional debris I was making a valiant effort to swim through.

We humans are so conditioned to hear the word cancer and associate it immediately with death. The Collective Consciousness of Cancer is a powerful force. It is a massive energy signature in the morphic field surrounding all of us. When a person suddenly gets thrown into the cancer arena, all the human alarms trigger, bells and whistles go off, and the SWAT team of the mind begins to assemble, readying for war.

No matter how strong my resolve and spiritual knowing, I found myself diving into fear of the unknown. Dammit! I was not happy about how this had evolved for me to learn and grow through. Yet, a part of me, the higher awareness of me, knew the truth of it. The dance I had performed through the grief of questioning my very life here without my beloved was choreographed perfectly.

I was extremely sick with nausea for several days but had the support of family and friends while navigating the news. I shed tears of disbelief and sadness with my daughter, my mom, and granddaughters as they held me in a loving embrace, unsure of what lay ahead. I could feel my daughter's fear, my mom's concern and my granddaughters' wanting me to be okay. We are all so connected through the energetic womb of our divine feminine natures, supporting each other in a deeply held family bond where words need not be uttered and love is all that exists. Love has a way of providing salve to the open wounds of the heart and the women I needed the most were right by my side as my new reality started to sink in.

I felt a little bit better after getting back home but my weight loss was clearly evident. I had a new full-time job, ME. I received an outpouring of loving support and, despite my initial need for privacy, I found myself no longer concerned with who heard the news since my family had all been apprised. I told my employer at the ranch where I worked that I would not be coming back and he was in complete support, offering whatever assistance I might need. I was given a light duty job next door to my business as a fill-in if I needed financial help. I continued to see a limited client base through my business, which always lifted my spirits and was healing for me. I had friends ready to offer me Reiki Energy Healing for all around healing support, Bioresonance Healing to assist deconstruction of mammary pathology, Vitamin C and Alpha lipoleic intravenous infusions to strengthen my immune system, Health Coaching with anti-cancer supplements and foods, Infrared Light Therapy to assist detox, Body Code and Emotion Code working with my body's innate wisdom and the underlying emotions behind the un-wellness, Massage to ease body ache, Pilates to keep body strength, Cranio-Sacral Massage to activate fascia and lymphatic flow,....the list was long and varied. All the while, I was stepping into the healing quest I had committed to. I knew in some fashion the journey would be part of my next book, a discovery into the deep waters of love, navigating through life and death in the most intimate of ways.

Staying out of the unconscious societal fear was not easy, as the collective energy is so strong around cancer it can overpower even the most resolute. I had no fear of death, not since losing Jack. In fact, the truth was I had often wondered how I could live without him. So leaving the earthly body was not my fear; it was the unknown ability of my body to do what it needed for physical healing while staying here on the planet that I found most unnerving. I did not want to live a life in which my life force vitality was slowly syphoned out of me. TRUST, I hear Jack say, trust.

On the afternoon of June 2, I had an appointment with the surgeon and oncologist. I spent the night at my daughter's home in Missoula to make it easy on me since the doctors' offices were there too. Besides, I knew being with family was good for my soul. Before my appointments, I sat on the grass in the sun, taking action on some self-care. I did my level best to stay centered, grounded, recognizing this was also part of the journey I would take; not knowing what was coming and stepping into trust. This was a biggie; trusting the unknown, trusting what was coming my way even though I knew it was not something I would have chosen consciously. I was aware we humans could all do more self-care, take care of ourselves at even deeper levels. We have the ability to show the way for others as we take steps forward on our own path. Our unique journeys have the capacity to impact those around us, those who need to feel seen and heard. The world needs me, the world needs us, the world needs love. I loved myself in those tense moments before walking into oncology; painting my toenails, sitting in the sun, smiling and sending love out to everyone, the cosmos, and praying.

The appointments went as expected. Standard protocol for treatment would be chemotherapy to shrink the tumor whose size was too large for lumpectomy surgery, surgery to remove the tumor, radiation, another round of chemotherapy along with hormone blockers. The inundation of information was a lot to take in and I was grateful my daughter was with me to take notes and ask the questions I may have forgotten. The next step was scheduling an MRI to get a closer look at my beautiful breast.

When I got home on June 3, there was a late afternoon thunderstorm. I have always loved the energy of storms and this was no exception. My roommate, Jane, and I sat outside, taking in the wildly breathtaking display Gaia was showing us. I felt as if the storm was symbolic of my life in that moment, the tumultuous winds, the rain starting to plummet to Earth, the thunder rolling across the landscape. Then, all of a sudden, I felt the urge to run barefoot out into the rain and dance. I danced the celebration of my life. I danced in the rain as a power stance, as if to declare my life path was not going to get me down. I would dance through what was to come with as much courage as I could muster; calling on Jack, my Guides, the Angels, Jesus and the Mary's, and God to be my spiritual dance team.

In the meantime, I decided to reach out to family and friends who were perhaps more distant, who were not aware of the circumstance I found myself in, so I composed a FaceBook post to send out.

Dear Family and Friends,

I have been in contemplation for many days now about how to share the information I am going to share. I decided I need to step into vulnerability with an open heart while asking for support for where my journey takes me. Just over 20 months ago, I lost my beloved, my soul mate Jack, to cancer. Just over a week ago I heard that word again only this time it was attached to my name. Wow! I knew my body had taken a hit with the shock and grief of losing Jack but the reality of just how much hit home with the words spoken...breast cancer.

So many lives are impacted by this word cancer and I certainly did not expect to hear it again so soon. I am still in the process of discovery, learning about: what my body is showing me; how the tumor is manifesting; how aggressive the cells; surgery is a given but not sure the extent; treatment options; alternative healing options; money; work loss; time involved in my healing process; finding the strength physically, mentally, and spiritually. All of these are unknown bridges I will cross as I step one foot in front of the other. I have had many moments when, deep in grief, I said to Jack, "I just want to join you. How can I live without you, my love? How can I go on? You are the other half of me."

Yes, in my darkest moments I have uttered those words. That is the depths of heartbreak from the physical loss of my beloved. But the core reality is this: despite how hard the last 20+ months have been, I am not ready to leave this beautiful planet. I have so much love to give, so much light to share, so much more to do on this journey. So I am asking my tribe (you who are reading this) to send me love, send me good vibes, send me prayers as I walk through healing this "un-wellness" in my body and move into a new paradigm of LIFE, LIGHT, and LOVE!

I know I will never lose Jack; he is always with me in our afterlife connection. But what I needed to do was to decide that life is worth living, even without him, and that I can move forward with complete divine love as my guide. I will be writing about my journey along the way and I plan to share updates as I go.

In the meantime, I will breathe in the beauty that surrounds me, I will be the most amazing mom I can be to my beautiful children, I will be the cool grandma who plays with her granddaughters, I will amp up adoration of my mom, brother, sister, and all my family, I will be that compassionate ear to my friends, I will dance in the rain, I will walk with God and my angels, I will channel my inner wisdom (and Jack), and I will still see as many clients as I am able to serve. MOST IMPORTANTLY, I WILL LOVE MYSELF through whatever this blessed life asks of me, honoring the soul that is known as Becki Koon.

Thank you all for your love and support. When we come together in love and compassion, miraculous things take place.

People were coming out of the woodwork to help me. I knew how blessed I was and never took the small moments for granted. Isn't it amazing how a life-altering diagnosis can bring everything into full laser focus, into sharp awareness, into a gracious gratitude for each breath taken!

I began diligently working with my Health Coach, Sharon, and we started a regime of supplements and Infrared Light Therapy to jump start my immune system and move into gentle detox. My goal was to continue to shrink the tumor by providing my body an environment of physical health along with the energy healing work I continued to receive from various practitioners. If I could shrink the tumor enough, they might not need to take the breast but could perform a lumpectomy.

June 6

Becki writes to Jack and he responds.

Well, my love, here I am facing my own challenge with cancer. I know you're doing all you can to get through, to support me, to assist me in what I face. I have been trying so hard to trust, trust that I'm OK, that I am healing, that I have the strength to walk these next few months with grace and spirit. I am having a harder time sensing you, feeling you. It is as if a damper is on my connection with you. The cancer, the "un-wellness" in my breast, has been there over the years, hasn't it, my love? I could go to all the places of I should have, could have, wish I had... but that is futile in this now, for the physical manifestation is here and I am now aware of it. It is a matter of trust, of faith in my soul purpose. I still believe I am here to share love, the deep and abiding love that is possible to experience on the Earth plane yet has its energy in the divine field of who we really are. I have to look at my desire to have you here, my yearning for your companionship here, my questioning if I really wanted to stay. And I finally feel like I know the answer. I do want to stay on this planet. I know there are others I can help on this journey. You are so full of love and support of me from where you are but I realize I also need that kind of love and support from here in the physical. I know you want that for me. Ours was always an unconditional love, one of wanting the other to excel in life even if that meant separation, letting go. My love, I am letting go. Not of our soul connection, but of my holding you so tightly, so hard that I have choked my own life force to dis-ease. I know there are other circumstances that have contributed, just like Dr. Matt said. But I know in my heart the tearing away of your physical expression here has been a key to this now moment. My life walk is not going to be what I would've chosen but losing you was not a conscious choice either and yet I know it was part of our contract together, our path to walk in a Divine sacred love and remember who we are.

Jack's Response

Step in to Becki, fully and completely. Who you are is not defined by me or our relationship but a beautiful compan-ion to your soul. You, Becki, need to trust that I am always here whether you feel me or not. My undying love for you never ceases even for a moment. It is in every breath you take, and every step you walk, and every moment you exist in form. I am and will always be your wing man and our walk together continues as long as it makes sense. But remember, as in life, when you are ready to completely move on, I will still be a part of you, an eternal piece of your evolving beauty and expression. You can do this, my love. Hold your head high and honor who you are. You are an angel to so many. I love you dearly.

Honestly, the rise and fall of internal emotions from sadness to acceptance was a constant reality, even though I was steeped in spiritual connection and knowing all was as it was supposed to be for my learning and growing. I continued to feel into the steps I could take and sought ways to empower myself while treading in the unknown waters.

June 7

I'm feeling the need to write some affirmations for myself and record them so I can listen to them being played over and over again. The power of my own voice with my own words will take my inner healing to a whole new dimension.

I am love and light.

I am the divine manifest into form.

I am health, wellness, and vitality.

I am the I AM in this form, this beautiful physical form.

I am strength manifest into the physical.

I am the one to share love on the planet.

I am the one to hold the beloved, divine frequency on the Earth plane.

I am the one to carry on, for my life force to fulfill my sole purpose perfectly and in harmony with my higher awareness.

My cells know how to heal. My body is wise.

I invite my DNA to work at top capacity, to invite my light codes in and to turn on and be recognized.

My innate body knows what to do to move out of dis-ease and "un-wellness".

Anything not in harmony with my best self is free to leave now.

I know miracles are real, and I create a miracle of healing that astounds the doctors.

Jack is always with me, loving and supporting me from where he is.

I trust my journey. I trust my path. I trust my faith in my life force.

I trust in God's love and the divine light path for me.

I am loved beyond measure and have so many things of beauty ahead of me.

My love knows no bounds. My trust has no borders.

I am divine will manifest into form and as such create the reality I seek.

I let go of those beliefs and actions that no longer serve me in my highest evolution.

I am love! I am light! I am compassion in action!

I recorded those statements into voice memos on my phone so I could play them anytime I needed. I put the recording on repeat and listened to them at night when I went to bed. I knew I was feeding my body, mind, and soul a miracle-manifesting food.

On June 8, I had a second Reiki session with Diana. I had been nauseous since the diagnosis of cancer. Not feeling well, not able to keep food down. I experienced withdrawals from the bio-identical medication I was no longer taking because the doctors asked me to stop immediately. My body felt out of sorts, my mind and spirit felt unknown due to the word cancer. My body was fatigued. As I lay there on the Reiki table, a powerful energy started to move through my body. It was the energy of Gaia, the living, breathing Earth. It was very strong. I heard the words, "I am holding you. I'll walk with you. Lean on me. This is our journey as you explore and understand working with the divine feminine principles." Then Diana moved to my uterus and started speaking directly to my uterus, to the energetic signature that still existed as my uterus. Gaia then talked to Diana. She said, "I am holding you in the womb of me. My womb has been hurt and damaged as well, so we are holding each other in that space of healing and awareness." Then Diana continued to remind my body that it knew how to regulate my hormones without the physical uterus. The consciousness that still existed knew how to balance my hormones. As she spoke to my uterus, my breast immediately recognized the consciousness of the uterus. It was as if a connection was missing. My breast tingled with awareness of the energetic connection now made, one of the keys to what my breast was looking for. It is an energetic connection, a consciousness still exists that had not gone away. Diana and I worked with Gaia and the Divine feminine. When Diana got to my feet, the energies flowed strongly through my body, down through the bottoms of my feet. I felt I had to breathe very deeply to keep it moving through. The waves of energy kept coming, flowing. I was told this is the healing, the healing I do not only for myself but also for others, the Earth, the Divine feminine, the Cosmos.

This channeling aligned with the card reading Barbara had done the night after I found out about cancer. I shared the news of the Reiki session with her because it was validating to both of us as we continued to dance with the spiritual wisdom being channeled.

June 8

Becki's Note to Barbara

Hi, Love. Headed into MRI early in the morning but just wanted to share that I had another amazing Reiki session today where more information came in related to the divine feminine and Gaia. Holy moly! This energy of the divine feminine and Gaia is real, my dear. I am going to try to remember all that took place, as it falls in line perfectly with your card pull. And the cool thing was that Diana did not know any of the card pull information beforehand. I will share more with you later. Love you. We are on track...with something big!

On June 9, I went into the hospital for an MRI of my left breast. My medical team needed to see more clearly what we were dealing with. As I was lying on the MRI table, I engaged in a pleasant conversation with the x-ray technician. When the dye used for the imagining entered my body, I tasted the chemicals in my mouth and could smell them as they entered my bloodstream. My body had become hyper-aware of what took place whenever anything entered it, including food. I reminded myself to breathe while I was positioned awkwardly on my stomach and chest so the breast tissue could be imaged clearly. It was not an easy several minutes as I perched, absolutely still, for the images to be shot. I contemplated how many people experience the very thing I was as I lay motionless, the exploration of a manifestation of un-wellness in the body showing up as cancer or disease.

On June 10 my spirit was taken into a Group Healing Session with a unique group of energy healers who gathered monthly to do distance healing on guests. Barbara invited me to be one of the guests that day so the group could send focused healing energy my way.

One of the members suggested it was really important for me to work with Earth energy, to hug a tree, to sit in the sun, to allow the energies of Earth to work with me, through me, supporting me.

Another healer suggested I allow Jack to be placed in a box, a box of love I could open anytime, but that allowed me to move forward with my life, not in so much of the grief in wanting connection with him. She suggested it was okay for me to place my channeling with him on a schedule and not have it be a constant connection, thus making it harder for me to want to stay on the planet.

A gentleman on the call suggested I was dancing Between the Worlds. He felt I was not clear if I wanted to stay on the planet or join Jack. He also suggested it was important that I decide clearly what choice I wanted to make.

A woman who had lost her husband suggested I set up a time that was our time to write, our time to channel. She suggested I book time with Jack, which would provide the gift of afterlife connection without the personal sacrifice to my own time and energy. Then, I would be co-authoring the book with Jack. She said I needed to stop punishing myself for not being enough. I needed to ground my spirit even more into my physical body.

Another healer suggested I work with the essential oils helichrysum, ylang ylang, and marjoram. She felt I was having challenges with the muscle of my heart. She strongly urged me to take care of my physical heart. Interestingly enough, that night I ended up having horrific chest pain. I woke up very concerned about what was happening and why my chest was hurting so badly. The fact that this woman picked up something in my chest amazed me and I immediately used the oils topically to calm the discomfort.

On June 11, I had a Cranio-Sacral massage appointment with Jody. We worked on my body and found one of my ribs had shifted out of place as I lay awkwardly on my chest getting the MRI. I had been positioned with the full weight of my body on my sternum. When they were scanning my left breast and I had to place my arms awkwardly overhead, it threw one of my ribs out near the sternum. Jody worked on my body and when the rib slipped back where it was supposed to be, the pain was relieved immediately. I was in awe of the abilities we have to pick up on the energy of others and the innate ability of the body to perform at its highest potential when given the right circumstance, such as a gentle, guided touch allowing the rib to move back into position.

Despite all my attempts at saying I was committed to wanting to live and move forward with life, deep down there was a rumbling, a rumbling in the deepest caverns within the psyche of me that knew the truth. On the surface it was easy to say I wanted to live, to share my life and continue the journey, but the internal rumble questioning otherwise grew so loud I could no longer ignore it.

I found I was dancing between the worlds, not really grounded in the physical realm, wanting to stay in the in-between, feeling the bliss beyond the veil calling me, haunting me. I knew I had a life-or-death decision to make. My physical body was gifting me the opportunity to make a choice. I had to let go of my yearning for Jack in the physical and non-physical at an even deeper, more profound level. I knew the rumble represented my internal questioning. Immediately, I felt my children, my family, my friends, my potential with another man, but mostly I could hear Jack pleading with me to stay, to love my life beyond him. In that moment, I found me and I knew the decision. With my heart completely open, exposed, and raw, I stood in front of his picture and spoke to him through broken sobs while I let the tears stream down my face.

June 12

I have to let you go, my love. Not a letting go of our divine, sacred love connection but a moving on in my current reality. I have to let go of my physical yearning of you in a way that challenges the very core of me, and yet I desire to live! I want my life here, Jack, and while I know you will never leave me, I want my life. I choose my life here on the planet. I choose to step into another love with a man when it presents itself. I am not done. Please help me to LIVE. God, please, help me to LIVE. WITH EVERY FIBER OF MY BEING, I CHOOSE LIFE! *Show me the way.*

I let the moment take me into full body release. I knew this declaration was my commitment to life and I called my daughter to share with her what had taken place. There was silence on her end of the phone as she listened to me pour my love out to her. She cried tears of joy because she knew her mom was struggling with the loss of Jack and her decision to live. Her biggest fear was that I would not choose life. We both felt relief, as if a large obstacle had been lifted out of the way of the path. This meant full steam ahead into the uncharted waters of the next few months.

That afternoon I had a Perelandra Flower Essence healing session with a dear friend. One of the activities she described hit a chord with me. She talked about another woman she had worked with who became cancer free by doing numerous alternative healing protocols. One of them was talking to her body about what the cancer was showing her but instead of writing with her dominant hand, she wrote with her non-dominant hand bypassing conscious thought into unconscious channels. I decided to talk to my body and see what she had to say.

June 12

Left-handed channel writing

What is the cancer showing me?

That I can heal. That I am a healer. It is inside of me. It is who I am. You know what to do. You just have to trust.

How did you as cancer come to be?

Your pain, your suffering, your loss of Jack.

How can I help you to move into a state of health? Not cancer?

Keep following your heart, your passion. Be who you are here to be. Live from your own heart.

I trusted what my body shared with me and I continued to seek options to support healing, following my heart for wisdom in the tough decisions I had to make.

I'd been contemplating the Divine feminine aspects within me, within my left breast. Assessing the releasing, the holding, the absorbing, the shifting, the transforming of the energy and the pain, the grief, the density, the shadow, the over-nurture, the lack of nurture, the hidden pain, the raw and exposed trauma, the healing, the holding, the honoring of it all! All of that is the lump, is the "un-wellness" in my body. My body knows what it needs. I am ready to receive all the abundance, knowledge, wisdom, and information my innate body has to share with me. The pocket of "un-wellness" is a gift in my evolution. A gift not only for myself but for others as I share the story of recovery, the story of the loss of many things on so many levels. And yet, the amazing journey to finding life again through it all.

June 15

I found myself on the massage table of a Reiki Master and Intuitive Channel named Eve. The session started out with a powerful surge of energy entering my feet that moved quickly through my body. The wave was strong. Eve felt it too and she was being guided to share that it was the energy of Earth, the Living Mother, who was showing me her support, her holding me in an energetic embrace. She was encouraging me to walk with her, in tandem with her. As the energy continued to move throughout my body, both Eve and I were moved to tears from the sheer beauty of Earth's compassionate and loving expression holding us. I saw myself standing on a cliff overlooking the sea. The wind was blowing my long hair and sheer gown as I gazed across the expanse of water.

Jack then made his presence known. He came to me, stood by my side at the top of the cliff. It was not the Jack I knew in this life; his physical form was slightly different but his essence was the same. He gently grabbed my hand and lovingly told me this is what we do. We come together in a sacred and divine love and have done so many times. Then he asked me to look out across the ocean and I started to see scenes as if on a television screen. Many different lifetimes came and went across the screen and he was telling me, yes, many times, many lives, many loves, many deaths. He told me we know death intimately and yet the love continues. He shared with me that it was not my time but that we would be together again in another now. He was encouraging me to live my life and allow love to flow to me, through me, and out into the world. Then he just held me through the rest of the healing session and I felt internal peace with all that was happening in my world.

The more I stepped into spiritual insight, the more empowered I felt in my journey to wellness. I felt the tumor inside of me getting smaller. I had a knowing that everything I was doing was working to help my body do what it naturally wanted to do, heal.

I had the opportunity for an unforgettable healing experience on June 19 when fifteen of our local Reiki Practitioners came together for a Reiki Circle. These circles are a beautiful energy exchange between practitioners who often do not take time for themselves to receive the healing energies they work with when helping others. This day was a full house with four massage tables set up and three to four people to a table. They all knew I was headed into surgery in a few days and the unconditional love present was permeating the room.

All the practitioners had time on the table and, at the very end of the event, they asked me to lie on the table in the middle of the room. All 14 Master healers gathered around me and offered me Reiki healing. There are no words to describe the power surge that took place and tears of joy ran as I openly received from the group. One of the gentlemen started to sing in light language and all of us were in an altered state of awareness as the divine light was shining on the whole scene. I could think of no more powerful way to walk into surgery than with those energies still flowing. We all openly wept, as the group felt the love of God present.

As my outreach for all-encompassing healing continued, I had the opportunity to work with an Energy Healer named Anna, who uses a pendulum to tap into the body's physical, mental, emotional, and spiritual systems. She was happy to report she did a medical protocol healing to make sure things ran smoothly during surgery and that the consciousness of all who were involved in the surgical procedure would be raised. She worked on releasing the trapped emotion of alienation I had picked up somewhere between Jack's cancer diagnosis and my own. She added a healing emotion of acceptance while releasing the emotion of anxiety about the current situation. She added the emotion of ease for the procedure. The trapped emotion of indecisiveness was released and the healing emotion of being decisive was added. She boosted and harmonized each of my major chakras for energy and raised my body's ability to fully receive healing. She also worked with the cancer cells to provide acceptance of cooperation for the survival of the body and to let go of their own self-interest for survival while neutralizing the underlying cause of the cancer. All these energetic healing protocols were in preparation for the days ahead.

June 29

Becki Updates a FaceBook Post

Hi Family and Friends. I wanted to update you on my journey. This last month has been the journey of a lifetime. Not exactly what I expected but one I walk with as much trust and faith in my life path as humanly possible. I am headed into surgery tomorrow for a lumpectomy of the pocket of "un-wellness" in my breast. Yes, it is called cancer. But what my body is showing me has wisdom beyond what I could imagine or can be shared in this short message. In ways, I feel more alive than I have felt since my beloved Jack transitioned from this life. Yes, I will be writing about the amazing experiences I am having through this process. What I can tell you is that the tumor has shrunk. My surgeon will go ahead and get whatever traces they find but my mind, body, and spirit are alive, well and in full healing mode. I am blessed to be a part of an amazing alternative healing community that I consider family and I want to thank you for all the support along the way. You have enriched my life and have shown what the power of our combined healing gifts can accomplish. Keep me in your prayers as I work with the surgeons and medical staff who will care for me tomorrow as we partner in my body's healing. I step fully into this life with love, compassion, and excitement for a future that looks brighter than I could have imagined. I am honored to be in community with all of you and I am excited to be of service to those who feel called to experience what I offer. My heart is full. Thank you.

June 30 was D-day, discovery day. I walked into the hospital full of hope and resolve. I trusted my medical team and my mother and daughter were with me the whole way. I also knew many people were tapping in and sending prayers, love, and light to my day. I could feel the cloud of protection around me and I absolutely felt Jack with me, right by my side.

The preparations took a few hours but once the surgery started, they told me it went like clockwork. My surgeon said he was able to remove the tumor. While he did not get as much of the surrounding tissue as he had hoped, the tumor itself had shrunk. I awoke from the anesthesia with a clear mind and no nausea. Thank God for the small triumphs. I knew I needed to focus on healing from the trauma my body had just gone through with surgery and all the medications that go along with a major operation. The amazing health practitioners I worked with had prepared me for this day. I also knew the gift in the energy field and the fact that my family, friends, guides, the Angels, Jack, Jesus, and God had all held me through the day. Another huge hurdle navigated and the uncharted waters had been sailed, at least to one of my destinations but there were to be other places to explore. I would patiently wait until my surgeon called with the results of the biopsy of the lymph nodes they removed.

Chapter 5

TREADING NEW WATERS

July 2021

*"My love, you are held by me in every moment,
your tears falling onto my cheeks as I hold you,
lift you, feel into your heart. I know life right
now is not easy on you but I am here, never not
here. Lean into me, breathe into me. Lean into
the divine, God's love for you."* Jack

T HE TASK AT HAND was recovery. I came out of surgery feeling strong and resolute with the choices I was making in my healing journey. I wanted to make sure I was honoring my body wisdom as much as possible. I understood the amazing potential of the body for miraculous healing and the challenge most prominent in my field was not losing track of my own internal knowing, falling into the abyss of fear of the unknown while waiting for the test results to come back on the lymph nodes they removed. Will they be benign or cancerous?

Despite having just gone through surgery, I found a vibrancy within, suggesting emotional relief for this stage of the treatment plan being over. I was aware all the prayers and energy attention had assisted my body and my medical team to move mountains for my highest good. I felt strong and connected to Spirit so decided to do a morning meditation.

July 1

Becki's Meditation

I just had the most amazing experience with Jack.

I went into my daily morning meditation with Lee Harris and was having a great experience raising the frequency and the vibration of my body. I was talking to Jack asking him to come in and help me raise my frequency, help the healing energies move through my body. As my frequency rose, I asked Jesus to come in and hold me as well and it was then I felt an intense vibration surround my breasts. I started to feel the cells in my body vibrate at such a high oscillation that my body wanted to go numb. My hands tingled, moving into numbness; my stomach, my sacral chakra, all areas of my body launched into feeling the movement of constriction through the tingling numbness coming on. The intensity was powerful and reminded me of the experience I had at Barbara's place in April. My body ended up at a plateau, immersed in the high vibration, all the cells responding.

At that point, I just wanted to feel Jack. It stirred up huge sexual desire in my body. I wanted him to make love to me energetically. So, I thanked Jesus and Lee, turned the meditation off and focused on talking to Jack.

I asked him to let me feel him, for him to make love to me energetically. That's when I felt the opening to him happen. I felt his cool essence surround me as his energy moved into me. My body became even more full of tingles and intensity and I allowed the waves of ecstatic joy to wash over me. When they subsided, my body became almost entirely numb. I went into a state of all-encompassing, utter calm. I lay in an absolute sense of peace and connection to everything, just breathing in and out of my body awareness. That lasted for several minutes as I bathed myself in that healing energy.

Jack again shared with me to trust. To trust in my journey. To trust in our divine love. To trust that he's with me, watching me, taking care of me, loving me from where he is. I have such gratitude and fullness of heart. He wants me to be full of heart and move forward in my life. He told me he will always be my beloved. The beholding of sacred love was our journey.

As I share the intimate details of my continued relationship with Jack, I realize speaking of our ongoing connection in the form of afterlife lovemaking will challenge belief systems, perhaps push buttons or set off alarms for some people. I may lose readers with the intimacy of this sharing but I could not in good conscience leave out this detail. Part of my healing was linked to my unending love connection to Jack and I had no doubt that, when enveloped in the higher frequency energies of the sacred and divine love I felt with him, my cells were healing. I could literally feel therapeutic benefits taking place in those intimate moments. It was a strange dichotomy to be in a position of letting go of him, my yearning of him, so I could move on with my earthly life, and still have this unfathomable relationship with him. It was part of the unique embracing of all sides of my life experience, the Yin and Yang of it all.

In one of the meditations I did with Jack, he took me to an island. We sat on the beach and he asked me to look out over the ocean. He said, "We are vast Becki, everything and nothing, light and shadow, but this, the US, what we do in the now, is sacred. Remember that, my love." He asked me, "What do you see?" As I gazed out over the expanse of ocean water, I began to see angels; the angelic realm opened and I was in awe of the beauty before me. He looked at me and replied, "The Angels celebrate our divine love." Then he took my hand and we walked along a path into the jungle where we came upon a bungalow. Once inside, we made love. Each time I felt the wave of energy cresting into orgasm he asked me to stop and hold there, to feel the elevations of energy in my body. As I held the continuously rising energy, he showed me a beam of light from our heart connection going out into the energetic grid around the planet. We were assisting Earth's ascension through our divine love. He told me I was learning a new energy technology and there were other couples who were sharing in this type of sacred love energy exchange for our evolution as humans moving into a more spiritually based life. Humanity as a whole was learning how to love as Spirit loves, to see the intercon-nection of everything through the eyes of compassion,

Christ Consciousness. He told me we were learning how to hold that high frequency within our bodies and when experiencing those vibrations of energy, the energetic signature of divine love and light radiated out into the world. I was in a state of all-encompassing, blissful peace.

I became aware that this elevated state of being was multidimensional and an aspect of my evolution into finding and healing Becki. I also recognized not everyone would agree with my learning; some would think I was crazy or possessed. Fear might be triggered in others. I had to let the understanding of other people's reactions, opinions, and judgments go. In my reality, in my body, in my soul, I understood my truth and I honored that others have their own path to love and light and to God. I knew my love with Jack was sacred, divine, of the highest form of energy two souls can experience and no one could take away my awareness of that truth. God was shining his light so powerfully within me I knew my future moments would be perfect for my soul's evolution, no matter the outcome. Besides, trusting my own wisdom seemed to be working.

July 3

Becki's Journal

The call I received from my surgeon on Friday night has me full of humble gratitude. My lumpectomy surgery went great, the surgeon very skilled, and the nursing staff all amazingly supportive. In 3 weeks' time, the tumor shrank from 2.2cm to 1.7 cm. That in and of itself was a blessing. The surgeon was able to get in and remove "the pocket of unwellness" while leaving as much of the breast tissue as possible. He also was able to target the nearest lymph nodes and removed 4 under my arm nearest the tumor. He was happy to inform me that the lymph nodes were clear of cancer cells and he also got clear margins around the removed tissue. While he had hoped to get more of a margin on surrounding tissue, he felt optimistic since the cancer had not spread into the lymph nodes. I am beyond grateful to my body and the amazing job it has done in teaching me what it needed to say.

I knew without a doubt that the alternative healing practices I performed in the month of June after the diagnosis had a tangible effect on the tumor shrinkage. Perhaps my body would have completely gotten rid of the rowdy cells on its own, as Jack said I could do. But I had also trusted my inner wisdom that said surgery was needed. I deeply honored my medical team for making the surgery be the best possible outcome it could have been. I was treated very well and, while I made some decisions contrary to their recommendations, I felt respected and heard.

There were so many people to thank, all the prayers and well wishes beyond the scope of my awareness. I thanked everyone I could. I realized the power we can wield when we come together in love and support. That truth showed itself in my reality. So many people were a part of my journey to a successful surgery, to wellness. I continued to move forward with my health regime. My mission on this planet was entering a new phase and I was not about to take the lessons my body showed me for granted.

My zest for life was enlivened and the sleeping tiger within me wanted to roar with power and passion for the life ahead of me. I was in love with the world and my spirit team, including my beloved Jack, were with me every step of the way. In fact, the surgical room was glowing with golden colors, the room full of angels and guides, ascended masters, and the grace of God.

I felt blessed by everyone as I navigated the twists and turns this spectacular human road asked of me.

And then it happened. My deep-feeling human self appeared on the surface of my emotional waters.

Just as I walked into strength and excitement about my future, another wave of sadness came crashing and overtook me. I deeply missed Jack, after my physical body had gone through so much. I found myself writing to him once again in my time of need.

Becki's Journal

Becki writes to Jack and he responds.

Jack, the tears are right at the surface. I miss you, especially now! I can't seem to find my strength at the moment. It is not easy to be going through the toughest challenge of my life without you here, holding me, touching me. I feel you, I feel your reassurance, but the ache of loss is very tangible today. I can't help how I feel. You and I, part of a whole package that feels depleted, worn out, the beautiful physical wrapping on our gift permanently torn into a million pieces. I have recovered some of those pieces, found their match, and I'm taping them back together the best I can. You, my love, are my rock.

Jack's Response

My love, you are held by me in every moment, your tears falling onto my cheeks as I hold you, lift you, feel into your heart. I know life right now is not easy on you but I am here, never not here. Lean into me, breathe into me. Lean into the divine, God's love for you. This latest part of your life is a continuation of our journey, your awareness part of the same story we share with the world. It is not your time to leave, Becki. Don't worry about your weight. Again, you are shedding the old Becki so you can move into the new with a whole new life force vitality. I will be by your side, my love. That was me this morning, reminding you of the powerful divine energy we share. Take it easy on yourself. The perfect weight will find you, but you do need to focus on water. Filtered, light-infused water. Use the tools you have. Trust water (my water bottle with the word trust on it) would be good for you to ingest. Trust in your body. Trust in your path. Trust that all is unfolding as it should. You are a blessed soul, my love.

You are blessed not from ego, but from heart, the heart of who you are, the heart of who we are, for you and I are one in the energy field. We are not separate but one with the energy of divine love. Hold that beacon of awareness. Others are coming to you. Others who share this journey of life, love, loss, and divine love will find you. I am helping.

It is part of the ascension, the holding of a frequency we can do no other way. Lean on those who can help ground you. Allow the ones who care to check in on you. Let those who love you, love you. It is healing for you.

Notice the small things, the butterfly that just flew past, the birds chirping, the slight breeze blowing, the warmth of the sun on your body, the clouds floating by. See the beauty all around you, my love. I get to see it through your eyes. Remember I get to see through you as well; the color, the mountains, the trees, the flags blowing in the breeze. Drink it all in. This is life and you are there to live it, my love. And of course, enjoy your human connections. You shine in the company of others. Let people fill your cup, okay?

I took in his words. I allowed my tears. I allowed my heart. I allowed my love. I allowed my healing to continue. Many of the healing protocols I put in place in June continued to support me. My full-time goal was walking the path of Life. It was a path I committed to, to the best of my ability. I had many friends and family who helped me by offering assistance, food, companionship, and I was full of gratitude for their kindness. My full-time job was recovery, recovery from so many aspects of my life. It had been only two years since Jack started to get sick, coughing with what we thought was a cold. So much to happen in such a short period of time. I was reeling in it all and keeping my head above water while treading in the deep waters of life.

I had been so steeped in my healing that I had not focused on Jack, was not consciously connecting to him as much as I had in the past. Perhaps my health was starting to wear me down, a long journey well taken. I started to wonder if I was losing the strong conduit I had with him. I was feeling shaky despite my fortune in health, family, and friends. The next book was looming in the background, a deadline making me feel unsure of my ability to make it happen. How would it be possible to find my way through all the layers of complexity I found my life expressing? Had I forgotten how to connect with Jack? Was a new friendship diverting my attention?

July 27

Becki writes to Jack and he responds.

Have I forgotten how to connect with you, my love?

Jack's Response

You have not forgotten, my love. You are the conduit for connection, voice to the amazing love we share, the beautiful divinity of energy filtered through your body and brought to Earth in the way we know and understand. We have done this many times. Don't doubt that. You were still growing into your essence, your light, your divine power, and you have to stabilize those energies, as they are more power than you are used to holding. That is why the diversion of a new friendship has been good for you. You need time to walk gently towards these moments, the work you are here to do for us, for others, for you, your soul. We are but one aspect of the multi-layered nature of this experience through your body. You are feeling stronger physically and I am grateful to your friend for helping you find that strength, feeling loved. Allow him to be your friend, my love. He does not possess the awareness you do when it relates to energy, and yet he has a beautiful heart. That is his draw for you. You connect to his tenderness, his soul essence, that is love. Allow yourself to continue to be open to your heart, to his soul heart. He will help you, as you have been helping him. It is OK. Be patient with yourself. You have your own life to live. Allow the unfolding.

Once again, I stepped forward bathed in Jack's divine love. I was amazed at how easy it was for me to forget how powerful my connection was to him. No wonder he was always reminding me to trust, trust, trust.

On July 31, I had a healing session with Jan, a Perelandra Flower Essence Practitioner/Healer. We were seeing what my soul brought forth as far as the flower essence connections. What needed to be taken care of on a deep level?

One of the first things my body brought forth to be seen was a Soul Spiritual Cause related to the Divine feminine wounding. It seemed I made an agreement at some point in my soul's journey to sacrifice for the collective feminine. I believed I needed to offer healing through my body, through my soul. Jesus came through during the session and we worked on the idea that I did not need to go through suffering anymore, I did not have to use my body to change the collective. I had compassion to offer others just by knowing and alchemizing energy. Jesus reassured me that all I needed to do was write about it, speak about it, and share the learning.

This came through as a surprise to both Jan and me but it was a concept that seemed to have been part of my soul's journey and discovery in the months prior. When I thought back to my session with Barbara in April, I understood why I felt such a strong connection to the rise of the Divine feminine energies within me. What Jesus showed me was a breakthrough for me and my body. I did not need to run the pain and suffering of the collective through my own body to heal and alchemize it into something different. I only needed to hold compassion to shift it. All I needed to do was understand it, write about it, speak about it, and share. What a blessing I was gifted and my body was thanking me.

The next flower essence that came up was from the Solar Ray Box, Number Seven, which was about balancing and stabilizing my energy field. It would help bring together the refracted soul heart links that had shattered into pieces, the pieces of awareness that needed to come back together as one essence. I felt this was my loss of Jack, my heart shattered into a million pieces when he left. As a result of working with this flower essence, my energy body would solidify and the foundation of my home base, my body, would become stronger.

The third flower essence to come through was a Zinnia, which was all about bringing me back to the state of joy and playfulness through innocence. I was to let go of self-judgment and societal judgment. It encouraged me to play the way little girl Becki would enjoy. So, what did I do? I danced!

Once again, the multi-pronged approach to my healing made sense to me and, while some people may have questioned my motives, my soul kept urging me forward. The learning I needed to heal with was to continue.

Jack's Message

To Becki

My love, you are sensitive and affected by those around you. You have been distracted but not alone. Remember, I am never not near you. We are love. We are love. We are love. Allow that to penetrate every cell of your body, my love. We came to show this, you the Earth beacon spreading this light in a very experienced way. Those who are in your field cannot help but be touched, as it should be. I was not to be the one on the planet. I was always going to be holding you up so you could be the spokeswoman to this energy. It is on track with the rise of the human collective. I will continue to hold you up, my love. Be strong.

Chapter 6

HONORING THE DOWNPOUR

August 2021

"Can you allow your tears of truth to flow as you feel the love of God? You are known, my love, and it is not about ego. It is about you understanding the depths of your divine connection. You walk the path of one devoted to the light, the compassionate love of Christ, with the devotion of one such as Mary Magdalene." Jack

ON AUGUST 1, I was offered the opportunity to speak at the Center for Spiritual Living in Hamilton, Montana. Despite my recent months' health journey, I jumped at the chance to be there with the congregation. The talk was entitled "Dancing Between the Worlds" and it was about the book Jack and I wrote, 20 Days Changed Everything. I talked about the death process and some of the amazing things that took place after Jack's passing, my connection to Spirit and God. I also spoke to the idea of life and death, the amazing rites of passages we go through as we navigate our lives. My journey with cancer was a part of my ever-evolving story. I said to the audience, "No matter how long I have here in this body, on this Earth, I will live it to my fullest, love to the depths I am capable, and be open to the joy and glory of it all."

The talk was very well received. At one point, I found myself choked up, tears welling in my eyes as I spoke about Jack. I took a breath in and looked up. There were about 50 people in the worship hall. When I scanned the room in that moment, there was not a dry eye in the place. I knew I had touched the hearts of those who were there listening to me speak and share, while radiating my love out to them. I knew without a doubt I was doing God's work. I was being bathed in a downpour of loving confirmation and I was grateful for my journey, for each precious drop of awareness that rained down into my soul.

Living a life steeped in alternative healing, I was navigating all available options and tools. One of the activities I did on a regular basis was free-flow writing. I have a thought or question in mind and then I open a channel through my heart center and allow the words to flow. When I write from the heart space, I know I am connecting to the divine, the God spark within me.

I had already been working with my body to understand what the cancer was showing me, not feeling at all upset with my body but trying to understand the energetics behind the manifestation of the tumor. It was no surprise that the shock of hearing the news about Jack and grief that followed his death played a role, but I wanted to understand at a soul level what my body was sharing with me. So, I went into meditation, picked up my journal and wrote my truth. Keep in mind that the words are my truth and not necessarily that of anyone else. We are all unique expressions of the God Force. I addressed my body and the cancer cells directly.

August 10, 2021

Channeling Becki did with her body and the cancer cells.

What are you here to show me?

Choice, you always have choice. You always have a choice to heal, choice to stay stuck, choice to recognize your divine power, choice to leave, choice to stand strong in your own journey, choice to listen to others' wants and desires, choice to not listen, choice to walk in joy, beauty, and sovereignty, no matter the circumstance of your life.

It is your awareness of choice we have shown you. You are listening and we, your body cells, applaud you for your wisdom and strength to step into awareness of what works for you. We want you to love yourself first and foremost. Do not overlook your body. You are learning and when the self-love becomes a constant state of being, we no longer need to manifest. Allow your feelings to rise and move. Allow the learning to flow out onto the paper as you share with others.

We (cancer cells) are part of a bigger whole, a collective consciousness that can move into a different state of being, but it must be done consciously and with intent. Thus, the healing can take place within (the body) as well as without (the collective energetic field of cancer). The learning is part of the collective desire to transform. (I was feeling that even the collective consciousness of cancer was ready to transform, to change the field of awareness).

Many use our type of cells to leave the Earth plane, a part of a bigger plan. But we are not to be feared, to be at war with. LOVE US INTO NON-EXISTENCE. Love us into a transformational energy that cleanses the heart and soul and changes lives. Complete love of self is the key. Can you love that completely, that fully, your body that shows you the pocket of "un-wellness" in your soul?

We only exist as a modifier of energy, a catalyst for the body, mind, and soul to shift, to change, to expand into something new. It's your choice - life, death, health, illness, healing, lesson, change, Love.

Everywhere I turned, I was being guided back to love, back to the heart, back to the divine essence that is the energy of the cosmos, the compassionate love of Christ Consciousness. I honored what my cancer cells imparted to me that day and have been loving them into non-existence every day since.

Sometimes the breaking open of the heart happens through tragedy, hardship, a dark night of the soul that catalyzes a reckoning. Other times, the opening of the heart happens through joy, laughter, the love of another, children laughing, blissful moments in nature. Of course, we all prefer what feels like a higher vibration but sometimes the biggest heart openings are the most challenging. Our task is to be willing to see it through the lens of divine love, to allow vulnerability. We all have choice in how we view the circumstances we find ourselves in. I knew I was in control of my choices and was willing to take full responsibility for those choices, despite what other people may think.

August 12

Becki's Journal

I had another appointment with the oncologist today. I told her I was not going to take the chemotherapy route. While she felt I was making a grave mistake, I appreciated that my decision was met with acceptance and grace. I was grateful the oncologist honored my decision, my truth. She wanted me to still consider radiation and hormone-blocking therapy. I felt empowered in my truth and yet I honored the fact that maybe I needed to remain open. So, I told her I would remain open to all other options. There is always room for more than one way, more than one choice, always more than one option if you're open to see it. I told her I would meet with the Radiologist and made an appointment to see him a week later.

Life was moving forward in a beautiful way for me. And the funny thing was, I had no idea what was ahead of me. I had no idea what it might look like or what it would entail. I knew the steps in the healing journey I took were more than just about me. The healing, the energy work, the writing, the sharing would all be part of a whole picture, a drama of one soul's life journey. I was growing more and more comfortable with that idea, more comfortable with the fact I had no idea what my future would look like. I was living this moment to moment, moment to delicious moment. It was all good.

My body continued to heal and there were times when I felt almost like my normal self. I maintained a positive outlook and Jack seemed an ever-present guard dog of my energy. People continued to show an outpouring of support while I maintained focus on listening to my body.

I never stopped seeking and following through with alternative healing. I found a woman who was an OMNIS Quantum Biofeedback System Practitioner. This system is an objective, non-judgmental device that senses the hidden stress energies within a body or space when connected physically or remotely. My four sessions with Ronda assessed my body's energy systems and guided us in quantum healing techniques in the unseen, yet very real, energetic fields of my body tissues. A friend gifted me another session of Bioresonance Distance Healing using a slightly different technique. I continued to have weekly Bioresonance Healing sessions with Hillary and Reiki energy healing sessions were a staple. I never stopped being dedicated to energy healing and spiritual coaching support.

The opportunity to host another Reiki Level I & II Retreat at my Wellness Center came up and Diana, Inge, and I jumped at the chance to offer this life-changing class. It never failed to be a catalyst for huge healing events to take place and I, for one, was more than ready to be bathed in those divine energies for a whole weekend. How blessed to be one of the teachers and to receive the gift of Reiki healing as well. I knew it would lift my spirits and fill my soul. I was not disappointed.

August 21

Journal Entry for Reiki Level I & II

Ocean of Holy Love Meditation

Jack met me on the path and we danced with joy-filled excitement as we headed to our familiar place. We saw golden hues shimmering off the ocean's surface as we ran and danced on the beach. We found our familiar log and sat down. Jesus and Mary Magdalene joined us while legions of angels were shining above the ocean's waters. Jack was reminding me to just be, that I needed to stay on Earth. They all held me in a swirling, healing energy. "Breathe the waves, watch as you create the waves. Love into Life, Becki," Jack kept repeating, "Love into life, Becki." Then they took me into the water and bathed me in the golden liquid. They poured the liquid gold over my head as they anointed me with holy love. I felt as if I was being baptized in the divinity surrounding me.

Then we all started to splash and play, laughing in the joy of the moment. Many souls were in the water playing and splashing around. A smiling Jesus reminded me it was great to play, to enjoy life. "Remember to find your childlike joy," Jesus said. After laughing and playing, Jack and I went to the shore and were basking in the sun when, all of a sudden, I was completely alone. They had all gone and I alone was on the beach. They told me I was to be on the planet, to share the higher energies, that they were never not with me despite how it appeared. I was to stay. I had to be okay with that.

The deeper meaning did not escape me. The last few months had taken me to depths in my own life acceptance that I did not know I had even questioned. Yet, at every turn it seemed Jack, Spirit, Jesus, Mary, and God were all reminding me I was to stay. I guess they felt I needed that concept reenforced, as if it was a key to my body continuing to thrive on the planet. My mission was being made very clear. Was I that hard headed? I laughed as some people who know me would say yes. Perhaps it was the Aries in me. All I knew was the baptism felt like a life-affirming cleansing of my soul so I could go forward on my quest.

August 22

Journal Entry for Reiki Level I & II

Healing River Meditation

Jack was with me at the beginning of the trail along the river. It was so beautiful, fresh, green, alive! I came to a bend in the stream and entered the water. The shimmering of the water surrounded me. Jack said this was my journey and I went on my own inside the water, swimming down, down, down into the womb of Earth. I felt held and guided, not at all concerned about the vastness of being on my own in Mother Earth. I came out of the water and saw an emerald city of pulsating crystals. Some souls came to me and asked if I would follow them into a temple, a beautiful emerald temple. The steps were an iridescent green and gold as we walked into the center of a large room. In the middle of the room was a huge slab of granite. I was guided to lie on the slab. Rites of passage, it felt like; death of the old is birth into the ecstasy of love. Six women surrounded me and began to pour healing energy into me. I had a flowing gown of green. Green was swirling all around as the women danced and moved the energies. Then the green colors were mixed with gold and purple. The women said to me, accept the healing. You are being held in so many realms. Breathe into who you are, the all-encompassing love that heals. You are sharing that love and service with others. Love the "un-wellness" you are experiencing into non-existence.

Again, I was reminded to love the "un-wellness" into non-existence. I knew I was not done with healing my body that had been through so much in the last several months. I continued to see alternative healing practitioners, worked with my health coach, had been to a Chinese Acupuncture Doctor, started to see a Naturopath and watched my diet. All these activities were intended to give my body the opportunity it needed to keep moving towards life.

August 22

Journal Entry for Reiki Level I & II

Placement II

As I lay on top of a grassy hill, a beam of light from the heavens shown down on me. The light was a brilliant golden-white and it pulled me into it. From within the light, I was taken up into space, the cosmos. Jack and Jesus were there. I saw the place around Earth was full of Angels and Beings of light. Jesus told me to don my robe, my robe of consciousness unique to who I am here to be on the planet at this time, the being I am here to be, to anchor love, compassion, Christ consciousness. He told me I am to seed divine and sacred love on the planet. My mind wandered for a little bit and then I heard them as a group say, "It is time, Miss Koon," just like my dear friend would say. I felt my friend there with us, part of my soul family, part of the journey. I just held that feeling of complete peace in the journey and then I went into a no thing space. Just resting into the no thing, no time, no agenda, the space of all that is. My lap became very hot, the only sensation I was aware of!

On August 23, I met with the Radiologist and once again had some tough decisions to make regarding my body. Could I remember to find that place of peace within as I stepped into the hospital's radiation department? I was extremely hesitant to jump on the radiation train and my body awareness was not giving me a clear signal while I conversed with the man who was to oversee my treatment. He reassured me I could stop at any time. It was my body after all and I could dictate how far I went, but he felt very strongly the best approach to my healing was a round of 16, full-strength sessions since I was not going to do chemotherapy. He was confident I had it in me to go the distance, even though I challenged the statistics he rattled off to me. My body was mine, unique, not statistical data or numbers or standard protocols.

And, yet...

I had to really step into my heart. What I recognized: it was my body, my decision, my life but I was not living my life in isolation. My children were very concerned about losing their mother to cancer and with my decision, their lives would be impacted. I could feel my daughter's fear of losing me. Could I step into the energy needed to walk in both worlds, allopathic and holistic? Could I love my children enough to hold the awareness of sacrifice for the greater whole, let go of my own judgments, and be open to the healing my body could do through radiating the tissue of concern, the surrounding tissue that may be holding seeds of cancer cells?

My decision came to me through my love of family. Would I have chosen radiation if I alone was the only consideration? Probably not. But then, my love for my children weighed in heavily for me as I stepped into the words that poured out of my mouth. "Yes, I will do radiation." I looked at my Radiologist and said, "But, if for any reason I feel it is not what I need to be doing, I will stop." His agreement led me to the reception desk where I booked my 16 appointments. I was to start treatment right after Labor Day, September 7th.

The internal awareness for me was knowing I was not inclined to do radiation on my own but when I looked into my daughter's eyes, I could see her relief in my decision. I could do this for my children, for those who loved me and were in fear of my leaving. I could swim in the divine ocean of light I was becoming so accustomed to seeking. I felt complete resolve in my decision. Besides, I had an amazing team of spiritual support with me no matter what route to healing I took. I was learning to embody love in all forms and the love for my children's mental, emotional, and spiritual well-being was honorable and without reproach.

My next question became, "Jack, Are you with me on this?"

Jack's Response to Becki

My love, honor the divine feminine aspect of your beautiful body in the now. Love the body that is finding healing, the breast that is transforming the energy of un-wellness, of grief, of the density of shadow, of over-nurture, of under-nurture, and hidden pain. Recognize the raw and exposed trauma you are healing, holding, and honoring. Honor all of it! The honoring of all of it is your task. You are doing a beautiful job, my love. Keep aware that your body knows what it needs. Allow yourself to receive all the abundance, knowledge, wisdom, and information your body has to share with you. The "pocket of un-wellness" was a gift in your evolution, a gift not only for yourself but for others as you share the story of loss, recovery, and love of life. I am with you always.

Chapter 7

DROWNING IN THE DEEP

September 2021

"If there was ever a time for you to step into trust my love, now is it. You're on the edge of the cliff and your life hangs in the balance. Please, trust it is not your time to leave. Our journey together in this divine love expression will continue with you on the planet and me here for as long as it is written." Jack

THE STEPS IT TOOK for me to walk into radiation with confidence and assurance cannot begin to be expressed in words. It was an energy of endurance for my body and a letting go into the hands of God, the outcome of the task ahead of me. My family and friends network was a gift I will be forever indebted to. Many people signed up to drive me to and from treatments, knowing my condition may be compromised, wanting me to focus on my body strength and not worry about to and fro.

The radiation team was amazing, a dedicated group of individuals with compassionate hearts, ready to answer any questions or concerns. The first step was to mark the target area, see how well I could hold my breath, and tattoo small dots on my chest to make sure they hit the right spot. It was a surreal few minutes to be placed on the table, arms positioned up and out of the way, taking a deep breath in and holding it, knowing that any slight movement could cause tissue to be damaged, like for example, my heart. I became keenly aware of my breath in a way that was laser focused. My job was to cooperate with the radiation machine by lying there perfectly still. Staying out of fear of the bizarre nature I found myself in was paramount. The holding of my breath became a practice of empowerment, at least in those moments of radiation exposure.

I was honoring my body the entire time, talking to my cells, and reminding them they knew how to heal, they knew what to do, and any residual cancer seeds could lovingly die off and move out of my body. I was reminding myself the people in the radiology department had my best interest at heart; they wanted my healing as much as I did.

The daily drive was enjoyable with my friends and I felt such loving support from everyone but, most importantly, I was seeing my daughter's fear subside, even knowing I may at any time choose to stop treatment. She knew I was giving it my all based on my beliefs and convictions. My family was behind me no matter what happened.

So, I continued to work part-time and see clients. My clients were my grounding, my semblance of normalcy while I walked the tightrope of maintaining wellness despite the fact I could feel the effects of the radiation fairly quickly. I am an energetically sensitive person and recognized the shift in my body, the depleting of my energy, early on. I also have a sensitivity to medication much like my father, not being able to tolerate chemicals or foreign substances in my body, often creating an allergic-type reaction. My father passed after chemotherapy and radiation treatments for esophageal cancer, the treatments more than his body could take prompting a heart attack.

The fact that a Master Reiki Training was scheduled four days after I started treatment was a huge boost to my soul. I knew this training was destined to be part of my divine recipe for success. What came out of the training was to be a catalyzing event to my very life force, a point of complete surrender to divine providence presenting another choice point. It would bring events into play that would rock the very foundation of my world.

I went into the weekend with excitement despite the fatigue already starting to filter into my awareness, my body beginning to feel the effects of radiation. My choice was to teach and participate to the best of my ability. That choice would hold consequences beyond my knowing and yet, as is typical for me, the meditations I experienced were profound.

September 10

Journal Entry for Reiki Master

Healing River of Love Meditation

I was walking in a beautiful redwood forest. The trees were lit up and alive, their energy reaching out as I walked. Jack peered out from behind a large tree and we proceeded to joyfully walk through the forest. We came to the river and it was beautiful, sparkling, full of energy. We walked along the path together in fun and laughter. We came to a place where we entered the water. Jack embraced me and my kundalini energy rose to meet him. We are carrying this deep love energy, he told me as we began to play in the pool of water, diving and rising. There was a waterfall and he took me to it. He told me to let the waterfall heal me, wash through me. As we embraced under the falling waters, Jesus and Mary Magdalene came. Mary took my hand and led me into a cavern behind the falls. We entered a large room. In the room were brilliant light, massive crystals, and the pulsing energy of Earth. She took me to the center of the room and I was soon surrounded by many other women carrying the Divine Feminine essence. I also saw men surrounding the outside of the room. Mary had Jack move into the center of the cavernous room with me. She shared that this was the journey, this was the path, Jack and I sharing this kind of divine love, with me holding the high frequency here on Earth working with Gaia. Jack and I embraced as my energy rose again. "This energy heals," she said. "It will heal your body. It will heal you. You are remembering what your spirit came here to do."

The waterfall I saw was spectacular and reminded me of the channel that had come through about water and my guides using the metaphor of water as love. I was awash in love. It was evident I was on a trajectory of love in all forms and expressions. I had danced with loss and grief through the downpour of my tears, at the same time learning to tango with the high energy, vibrational ecstasy of afterlife connection and lovemaking with my beloved Jack. For me, the energy of my sacred essence and divine love was formed in the same breath as God, not separate but part of the all I was becoming.

September 11

Journal Entry for Reiki Master

Ignition I

My heart was racing very fast as I went into the Ignition. I was feeling my body, fully in my body, no out-of-body awareness, just fully embodied. My heart kept racing and then suddenly it went heavy, as if something was on my chest, sitting on my chest. I felt completely heavy in my body, weighted down. As I continued to breathe into my body, the heaviness began to lessen and eventually a calmness came over me, my body feeling a sense of peace. I had full awareness of the density of my body, the physical constriction experienced by my spirit in the form of Becki. I found a level of complete acceptance for the adventure of being human.

When I came out of the first Ignition, I was conscious of my body. While I trusted the process, I could not help but wonder how much was related to my spiritual awareness and how much was my body responding to the event of radiating tissue and feeling the gravity of what those cells were going through. Was that the weight creating heaviness in my heart? My goal was to see beyond my human limitation and to view the circumstances from a higher and broader perspective. Could I remember to love my body into wellness?

September 11

Journal Entry for Reiki Master

Ignition II

I saw a golden white light moving down, swirling into my hands. It entered my heart and filled my body, all my cells lighting up, the kundalini energy within me rising. Jack was there along with many ascended masters. I was told, "In this energy you are one with us. We are one vibration." The energy rose and receded in waves as they just kept asking me to hold and ground that light onto Earth. "Keep healing, grounding, holding the higher vibrations of light. We are all one!"

The learning I had gleaned through the school of hard knocks was this: high vibrational frequency has the potential to heal. While being human is a complex and multi-dimensional experience, I knew, with every fiber of my being, we humans can access a miraculous life. When I allowed myself to step into the higher-level energies of light and vibration, my body took health and wellness to another level. I could feel the shift in me. What escaped my conscious mind was the fact that another experience would catapult me into an even deeper understanding of choice.

September 11

Journal Entry for Reiki Master

Ocean of Holy Love Meditation

When I was resting on the log, Jack came and sat with me and we gazed at the Ocean of Holy Love. This is our time. Mary came up to me and lovingly grabbed my hands and led me to a circle of women standing in the ocean water. They were celebrating birth. Then I found myself with another group of women in the ocean and they were performing a celebration of death. They showed me a vision of me leading those ceremonies. It was very honoring and sacred. Then I found myself on a high cliff above the ocean and I saw small boats full of souls making their way on the voyage to the afterlife. I was dancing and singing to them from the place I stood. Jack joined me and we were honoring the souls as they journeyed. I then saw many vignettes of lifetimes where I assisted the death of others, some in celebration, some in complete heartache, many with Jack and the death passage we have known. The vision ran the full gamut of the death experience. They were reminding me of the service of passage, of that divine love shared in the journey of transition. "You have known great love, great loss, and great service." The women told me, "We are like the waters, our blood the same as the ocean. Allow your blood to aid in the flow of the life and death cycle, Becki."

Even though I was not clear about the meaning of my blood flowing as the waters, I felt the impact of the message in my body, in my soul. There was a mysterious and enlightened meaning I felt would unravel more and more as my life moved forward. The mystery of the spiritual energy I was navigating pulled me onward with a fervor I would need in the days to come.

September 12

Journal Entry for Reiki Master

Ignition IV

I saw a purple flame engulf my heart, burning brightly. It grew slowly until my entire body was a flame. My hair flaming out, away from me. Jack came to my side. He too was a flame. We merged into one beautiful all-encompassing flame. My energy began to rise as the frequency of love spread all around us. Jesus and Mary came and they too were flames of holy fire. They then took us deep into Earth, to a huge space. As we were flaming and glowing, the energy began to move up through the earth to the surface and then I saw the energy like a volcano spreading light and flame across the entire Earth surface. The planet became engulfed in the holy fire flame; it was as if we were all sending out the flame of Christ consciousness. As the light and the flame covered the planet, everyone was able to reach up and pull in the energy of the Christ flame, the love available. I continued to vibrate in the higher energies of Divine love. Trust the journey, the burning of what no longer serves you. You are a key. We hold the key.

Sometimes choice is fraught with the inability to see clearly what our intuitive nature is guiding us to experience. When the training started, I was in a situation where my inner voice spoke to me and I ignored the inner wisdom. I so wanted to teach this Master class and yet someone attended the class who did not feel well. My immediate reaction was to excuse myself from teaching; there were other teachers available who could take charge. My intuition said I did not need to expose myself to vulnerability while I was in the middle of dealing with radiation for cancer. Then some part of me rationalized away my intuition and my sense of responsibility and desire for my own experience overrode my inner warning.

I grew weaker as I continued radiation treatments but my spirits remained up. Several days later, one of the class attendees came down with COVID. I found out I had been directly exposed to COVID right before I headed into what would end up being my last radiation treatment. I was feeling sick and my skin was starting to blister across my chest. As soon as I got home, I did a home test for COVID and it showed negative. But by Saturday morning on September 18th, I was not in good shape, feeling sicker and sicker. I knew it was much more than just the radiation my body was feeling. I went to the hospital to be tested and sure enough, I tested positive.

I had learned by now to be resilient, walking through many trials while maintaining composure, balance, my choice for life moving forward a gift from God. But even with all the strength I felt within me, I began to question whether I was going to be okay. Was my body going to have what it needed in energy reserves to overcome this next hurdle? By Monday, I could not move or get out of bed. My entire body was aching so horribly, I just lay still, drowning in the deep waters of pain, unable to keep anything in my stomach, not even water.

The human body is phenomenal in what it can endure. It brings to mind stories of human endurance, the ability to overcome extreme conditions and move mountains toward a great purpose, often survival. How much of what we face is directly impacted by our thinking, our capacity to empower the higher-level vision connected to something greater than ourselves. The power of the spirit that moves through us, that animates the body, can become the lifeline to save us from drowning in our own suffering. On the flip side, our thinking can tarnish our thoughts with negative outcomes, buying into a collective story that sucks the life force right out of the body. My thinking was becoming tarnished with the collective fear surrounding COVID. Was it not enough that I was dancing with the manifestation of cancer and radiation? Did I really need to sink into the collective whirlpool of fear around COVID as well? My mind was lost in swirling thoughts of uncertainty. My solid connection to Jack and my spiritual team was full of static and spotty reception.

My family and friends jumped into action. My aunt had contracted COVID and was able to receive the antibody infusion early on in the pandemic. It had helped her immediately. She could feel the antibodies going to work even before her infusion was finished. The infusions were not easily available in my location but luckily, an old family physician where Mom lived was offering them. She set up an appointment and, with the extenuating circumstance of cancer and radiation, he offered to see me as soon as possible, if I could get to him. The kind man had been my father's doctor and held a special place in his heart for my family.

The hospital where I was to receive treatment was five hours away from my current home in Montana. Mom was ready to drive to my place, pick me up, turn back around and drive us to her home in Rexburg, Idaho. It was then that a dear friend offered to drive me and I took him up on his kind gesture.

By the time my friend and I left on Tuesday, I was not in a good place. My body was aching so much that every time the car went over a slight bump, moans would automatically be produced. He was deeply concerned about my level of comfort and knew the car ride was uncomfortable on my body. Nausea was coming in waves. My lungs were not where COVID landed in my body, it was my stomach and intestines. I was quickly becoming dehydrated. On top of that, I was also feeling the burn of the blisters on my skin from radiation exposure. I was extremely weak.

We arrived at my Mom's house in record time. I crawled into bed and did not leave until it was time to see the doctor on Wednesday. My friend stayed in the area until he knew I was in good hands and safe with family. I will be forever grateful for his care of me during my time of unwellness. From the time I met him in April, through my cancer diagnosis, he was always ready with food, dinner, or company when I needed it. Love through friendship cannot be underestimated, agape love, the highest form of charity.

The doctor was very kind. I reminded him he had delivered my daughter 35 years earlier at the very hospital where life would be infused back into my body, giving me the boost needed to survive the virus that seemed to be taking me down a path not even the cancer did.

The infusion was scheduled for Thursday and I was able to walk in under my own steam, albeit very slowly. My mom had been making sure I was getting liquids and some small bits of food so some of my strength had returned. As I sat in the room receiving the infusion, I offered thanks to God for giving me the opportunity to be sitting there, receiving the life-giving antibodies when so many others had passed with this diagnosis. When I left the hospital, I felt a hunger pain move through me and was craving a cheeseburger, of all things. Mom, surprised, gladly drove through a fast-food drive-up window and ordered me a cheeseburger. It was the first food I had kept down in days.

Once back at mom's home, my body continued to experience the sickness. Recovery was not going to be as fast for me as it had been for my aunt. I was still in such a weakened state from the radiation and months prior that for the first time, I felt my life was hanging on the edge.

September 24, two years to the day that Jack passed, I was crying, talking to him. "Jack, I'm not sure I have it in me to do this, to find the strength to recover. Is this my time to leave? Am I really going to die because of COVID? Please, my love, help me understand why. I feel more broken than ever before." I felt a gentle wash of love move through me and heard him say, "I know you are down, my love. I know you miss me, but it is not your time. You will find your strength. Trust in God's plan for you, for us, for those you will help. You are going to be okay."

My mom had taken up the mantle of the mother bear protecting her cub and together we endured some very humbling, human aspects of a physical body not functioning well. She never left my side. My mom has always been my greatest caregiver. I was born pre-mature and my tiny little body was full of fluids in my lungs. I was placed in an incubator and doctors informed my parents I might not survive. My mom held vigil then, praying to God to let me live, "I will be the best mom I can be. Please God, let her live!" Not only did I survive, but under her love and care, I thrived. Now, she held the same unbreakable, loving strength for me while I was finding my way back to life.

I was being nursed back to health by my loved ones here and in the afterlife. I had to remind myself to keep breathing into what little life force I felt. My son came to be with me and when he drove me home, back to Montana, he stayed another week to make sure I was out of the woods. Outside of a trip to the ER to get fluids for the continuing nausea and dehydration, I was slowly coming out of the fog.

Jack's Message to Becki

"My love, you are so much stronger than you know. Your path is being guided by the light of awareness into divine living, letting go, and trusting. You have had to trust like never before. Deep within you is the remembrance of who you really are as an angel walking on Earth. Feel into that during times of weakness. Humans are so much more powerful than they know or understand. And, the realms of Spirit are working with each of you, every step you take, no matter how hard the circumstances seem. Remember to seek, ask, look to your divinity for support. You, Becki, are my beloved. I will always be by your side, even when you are not able to feel because you are lost in your humanness, your beautiful humanness. Embrace it all, my love. You will find your way."

Chapter 8

THE RIVER FLOWS

October 2021

*"The energy of divine love never diminishes!
NEVER! It only knows expansion, growth, and
evolution." Jack*

HOW MANY DEFINING MOMENTS can one person have? Perhaps, as many as it takes. I found life was presenting me with many choice points, moments where I could step into a clearer, more empowered version of myself.

After I spent several hours in the emergency room getting fluids to counteract dehydration from the overpowering nausea that kept interest in food or fluids at an all-time low, I had a pivotal moment. I was lying on the hospital bed, by myself, talking to Jack. The room was freezing cold and the fluids running into my arm chilled me even more. The hospital ER was busy and I lay there for long periods of time with no one around, listening to the ticking of the clock on the wall. Why didn't I grab my cell phone? My migraine was blurring my vision anyway, I reasoned. My heart was aching for Jack to be by my side, not in spirit form but in flesh and blood. I was shedding tears of sadness, realizing the one person in the whole world I wanted standing by my side and holding my hand was not there physically.

At home the next day I began to feel a bit stronger. It was now October. My son was going to spend a few more days with me until the weekend and then head back to work. The weather was nice and I enjoyed sitting outside in the sun, soaking up the rays while I let my face feel the warmth and breathed in the fresh air. I was on my way back.

Something happened to me in the days after the ER visit. A well of energy started to build and I began finding an internal powerful resolve beyond anything I had recognized over the last several months. Perhaps it was teetering on the razor's edge of death with COVID, or a reckoning with my needs and desires; I don't know. The power surge was not like anything I had felt when dealing with cancer. It was something so much more. It was a declaration for life I would come to call COVID Courage.

Warning: Do not read this paragraph if you have a sensitivity to swearing; if so, my apologies to you. I was not normally a person who used swear words, but I felt this commanding, fiery energy pulse through my veins and I was not going to pussy-foot around anymore. It was the evening of October 6, when I sat up in bed and yelled, "Fuck It! Life is too fucking short to not live it! I am here to live my life and by damn, I am going to live it! Do you hear me? Jack, I love you but I am going to claim my life.

I don't care who doesn't agree with what I do or how I go about it. Fuck 'em!"

I called a friend and shared this new found strength, still cussing like a sailor. I felt like Supergirl being bathed in magnificent human strength and I would no longer accept the various aspects of other people's version of kryptonite into my life.

Yup, I called it COVID Courage.

A sudden cancellation in my new Naturopath's (Dr. Mark Kelley, Naturopathic Doctor, LAc) schedule opened on Thursday, and I was able to take that appointment to see him. We began to strategize how we were going to support my physical health and work with my body to provide the optimum environment for healing and wellness going forward. I went in with my new-found courage and he was impressed with my resolve. He suggested I work with another Naturopath we both knew (Dr. Matt Schlechten, Naturopathic Doctor) who was an expert in the cancer arena. I had already worked with Dr. Matt and trusted his experience. Between the three of us, we would be a great team. I made a call to set up an appointment with him as well. I was pooling my resources and I felt empowered.

In the morning hours of Friday, October 8, I had a beautiful meditation with Lee Harris and could feel the kundalini energy once again rising in my body, in my cells, in my energy field. I was so ready to connect with Jack, Jesus, and God. It was a beautiful reckoning with my body. I was answering the call to life, coming out of the fog, and I felt Jack so strongly guiding and encouraging me along the way. I was ecstatic to feel my beloved again, as the connection had been harder to feel while I was so sick. I was remembering more of who I was and stepping into my energy, my knowing and my connection to God. I was full of grace and humility for the blessings I had been given.

That evening my friend Adele came over and we did a meditation with a friend of ours, Ambujam Rose. Her group power healing was about releasing what no longer served us and stepping into those energies of higher awareness, the higher aspects of what we are here to do. This healing was right on track for releasing even more of what I needed to let go of, the paradigm of sickness. We were called to recognize the God within us and who we really are as divine beings in human form.

On Saturday I stayed with my friend Jane at her cabin. We had a great time, dinner, dancing, laughter, and fun. Once again, I was feeding my soul with life force energy, the things that lit me up. On Sunday we participated in a guided meditation with Lorie Ladd. In this meditation, we met our guides and, as our spirit guides approached us, they asked us to give them something we wanted to release, to let go of. Then they asked what we wanted to receive in return. I knew right away what I wanted to hand them, the unwellness in my body, the cells that were operating at less-than-ideal capacity, any remaining cancer cells. I asked my guides to please take the unwellness from my body through love and light. I handed it over to them. In return, I asked to receive health and wellness, vitality, and aliveness.

I began to understand: for me to move on in life, I needed to understand and see some of my human relationship in a whole new light. I needed to pull away and set boundaries with some; I needed to be clear and open with others; but most of all, I needed to honor relationship to myself, who I am, what I need and want and what I deserve. None of this was to come from a place of ego but from a place of compassionate, loving awareness and honor.

When I got home Sunday evening, I began contemplating relationships. We are so driven by relationship while in human form. Often our greatest challenge, yet greatest growth, comes to us through relationship with another. I knew my new-found declaration would mean a moving forward in life in a way that involved another man coming into my life, one in the physical realm. Jack had been sharing with me all along he wanted me to be happy, wanted me to live life here, wanted me to move forward in love. Now more than ever, I felt the truth of his sharing, looking at my belief systems and patterns, assessing whether I had something getting in the way of that moving on.

All this contemplation, though, just stirred up feelings of wanting to connect with Jack energetically again. Was it possible to be in human relationship with another man while continuing to have an energetic relationship with Jack? Was this too strange to consider? Was it too selfish on my part? Would it be fair to the other man? Was it possible to have it all? Would Jack leave me if I did move into relationship with another man? All these questions were running around in my head when I realized what I needed in this now moment was to feel Jack, to have the healing energy of my connection to him running though my cells, raising my vibration to meet him in the frequency of divine love, radiating and expanding that divine love frequency out into the world, healing not only my body but the energetic field of the cosmos.

I talked to Jack and invited him to come to me, to love me in the way only we could, by reaching across time and space, dissolving into the divine sacred light of oneness we shared. I thanked him for our beautiful connection. I talked to Jesus, Mother Mary, Mary Magdalene, God, my guides, my higher self, and said to all, "Show me what it is I am here to do, to continue to do. What is the piece I am here to offer through all this life experience? Show me the way." My night was blissful. In that moment, I honored my connections, walking in a divinely purposeful life, my life a walking prayer.

I had stepped into the flow of my life. When I awoke on Monday morning, I participated in a phone conversation with a woman who had lost her husband in August and was in grief. We shared a few tender moments of recognition and support. I held an energetic space for her to feel held and heard. I thanked God for using my body and life experience to be the conduit for another's comfort.

With confidence, I made a decision and phoned the Radiologist to inform him I was canceling the rest of my 7 radiation treatments. While he was concerned about my decision, he was respectful and encouraged me to keep a close eye on my breast health going forward. I thanked him for his care and honored his concern for me. He told me he was there in the event I changed my mind. Again, I felt myself becoming stronger the more I walked in integrity with my internal knowing and truth.

Only an hour after I visited with the Radiologist, I received a call from Dr. Matt. I had been trying to catch up with him for a few days. He had been trying to catch up with me as well. He was wondering if I could get in to see him after lunch. The flow of the energetic river was rolling fast this day and I was able to say, "YES, I will be there!"

Synchronicity is an occurrence of recognizing the perfect timing of events as they unfold in divine order and, since I had made my declaration, life was presenting itself as magical. I paid attention to it all. It was as though the lens of my sight cleared and I now saw through enhanced rose-colored glasses. I was beyond grateful.

On Monday, I walked to a nearby restaurant to have lunch with my friend Jane and, to my surprise, noticed Dr. Matt sitting at the food counter having lunch. He had been in town at least two months and I had not seen him anywhere around. Yet, when his energy was in my field of awareness, here he was. We laughed at the glaring inter-relatedness and he said, "I will see you in a few minutes."

As I walked into his office, I immediately felt an internal nod of validation. He said it was a good thing I connected with him today because this was his last day in town; he would move out of town after our appointment. Okay, I was used to seeing the magic in life but the synchronicity I was experiencing was awe-inspiring. In fact, I had phoned him to tell him about my cancer diagnosis, knowing full well I would be leaving a message because I thought he was in Mexico, but I heard his voice. Normally, he would not have picked up the phone. It was his birthday and he expected to hear a happy birthday from me, which of course he did. You just can't make this stuff up!

We proceeded to consult about my cancer journey, my COVID journey, my health journey, my mental, emotional, and spiritual state of being. He had been working at a cancer clinic in Mexico and had treated thousands of patients. His knowledge base was one I trusted. He talked about the different levels of treatment we could consider going forward. And then, suddenly, he asked if he had ever muscle tested with me using a type of kinesiology. I had worked with him years earlier on some other health issues. Being the energy healer that I am, I was elated. Yes, we had done muscle testing with me in the past. I was excited he was going to use my own body wisdom to help us design a program specific for me. He was the only doctor I worked with who used muscle kinesiology to tap into the body's innate knowing. Once he asked my body what it wanted, he put together a program of support specific to me. My body was not just standard protocol but a unique expression having its own desire. He was surprised at a couple things the muscle testing revealed, hence the reality of my unique life force. The more we talked, the more excited I got as I began to recognize working with Dr. Matt and Dr. Mark was a key to my physical recovery.

He mixed an intravenous infusion which my body took in with ease. As I sat there waiting for the bag to empty into my veins, I read him the channeling I had done with the cancer cells. He was fascinated and understood I was approaching my cancer journey in a highly unique yet powerful way. Of the thousands of patients he had treated, he said no one had the perspective I espoused. My body continued to take in the infusion with no trouble, wanting what he had mixed up. I informed him I would be writing a book, sharing the journey from a different perspective, a different version of stepping into self-love, body love. I would be writing about what we were doing. He looked me in the eyes and said, "Becki, if you are in, I am in. We are going to do this. Let's do this. Are you with me?"

As we bumped knuckles, I said, "Absolutely! Let do this! I am ready to do what it takes to make my body well!"

For the first time in months, I felt there was a key to a door I was opening and walking through, a door into my wellness in the physical, but also emotionally and spiritually working with the energetics of my being. I had a doctor who understood and would work in tandem with the energetic side of the equation. I would bring the energy healing piece and he would bring the physical. For the next three months, I would work closely with the two doctors who would provide access through the door.

I left his office feeling like I was walking on clouds. I came home and got on the schedule with both doctors for infusions and treatments going forward. My commitment was an intensive three-month journey and I stepped in without reservation. I intuitively knew I had been handed a key, a key to my transformation in a way that empowered me. I was walking in alignment with my higher self, my God given divinity, and no one could deter me, not even collective fear. I knew the money would come, the healing would happen, the spark of life in me was soon to become a blazing fire I would share in service to humanity. I could feel Jack giving me an energetic high-five.

I cried in complete surrender to the gift of my prayer being answered so quickly. God showed me that day the power of prayer, the power of divine love to walk us into our life, into our purpose. The river of love I swam in was taking me toward a vast ocean of expansive, compassionate awareness to be shared with others. My task of self-love was so strong the vulnerability of sharing the raw, intimate details of the journey would become the salve of salvation for me and others who find me. I could not deny this was my path, this was my journey. How amazing was it that I would get to hold a level of power, of energy, of awareness and healing, then share it with other people.

Dr Matt had told me the most powerful occurrence they found at the clinic in Mexico was when a person with a certain type of cancer was able to talk with another person with the same type of cancer and they offered support to each other. Powerful healing could take place when someone had success and walked away saying, "I am cancer free!" When someone was able to say that and be the example for others, it gave other patients hope. It helped them see a different way. It helped them understand they too could do it. What if people had the opportunity to not be at war with their body but to love their cancer into non-existence? That is a paradigm shift of huge proportions. It is not for everyone by any stretch. But there are those who feel an energy within, needling them to try a new way, to look at it from a different vantage point.

I was being guided by a power greater than myself to write. I felt an aliveness in my body I had not felt for months. I was here to share this information, to be of service in a way that is unique, different, part of the special, unique spark that is Becki. I felt so honored and blessed knowing my life was going to move forward and I was going to be okay. During the preceding week, it was as if switches in me kept being tripped, over and over. I was changing the channel into a new version of life.

Having COVID changed me. It took me to the brink of death but out of the ashes arose a power to take charge of my life and drive the boat, my divine spiritual team co-piloting with the destiny map leading us on down the river, trusting the compass of love. The mantle of my divine light that could see and was connected to everyone, the divine self that knows we are all in this together, the divine oneness that recognizes we all have something to share, the divine love that understands we are stronger together than individually, was the truth I was choosing to exude. The truth of Becki, the spark that flames out and ignites the flame in others until we all burn with the ferocity of a blazing fire of compassion that transforms lives, that changes paradigms, and shifts the worlds.

Interesting how I thought I had claimed my life after losing Jack and finding out about the cancer but after COVID, I really fucking claimed my life! Because, out of claiming my life, I share the journey of divine love, compassion, self-awareness, and self-love, leading beyond the label of grief, beyond the label of cancer, beyond the label of COVID, beyond the label of unwellness. My guides handed me health and vitality and I took it. I plan to hand over unwellness, again and again if I must. What a life! What an amazing life to have and to share with others with the goal being inspiration!

Infusions twice a week were to be my new normal. I traveled when it called for travel, I arranged schedules to meet the needs of the treatment. The entire time, I felt alive and so full of hope.

The first round of cancer bloodwork showed a slightly elevated level in the breast marker and within normal range in the two other measures. We would monitor the breast marker closely.

In the meantime, life continued to move forward. I started to open my client days again. I worked a part-time job nearby and was preparing for a couple interviews about my book, *20 Days Changed Everything*. My new normal was an intricate dance between my health, my business, my social life, and what felt like my life purpose.

One morning before work, I needed to get something from under my bed. I felt a small object I thought might be a dropped vitamin that had rolled under. When I pulled it out, It was a small stone from the ANDEANSol Rocks: Pathway to Light book and dousing stones. This set of stones were an instant connection for me and the beautiful woman who created the stones and wrote the book, Christina Oss LaBang, wrote the forward in my book. The minute the stones hit my hands, my body chilled and I could feel the power of Gaia radiating in me. Somehow, one of the stones, the Wild Fox, ended up under my bed.

Of course, the first thing I did was go to my set of stones in the other room and see if the fox was missing. To my surprise, the stone was there, not missing from my set. When I thought back on the places I had been with the stones, I could not recall having them in the bedroom for months.

Magic sometimes happens through the moving of objects in my life. Even though it doesn't happen often, I have been aware of physical matter moving numerous times and my guide, Micah, was often behind such events. My body was in chills as I realized there was no explanation for the stone being where I found it, let alone materializing when the stone in my set existed, in its proper location. The Wild fox is all about expecting the unexpected.

I was so curious about the meaning, and my first thought was my health.

I decided to do a little detective work and explore with my guide what this experience could be related to. I went into channel with him and asked if it was related to my health: no. Was it related to relationships: no. Was it related to my work in the world. YES! I was fascinated. It fell into alignment with what had been coming through me recently, the guidance I was receiving from God. The interesting piece of life being presented was that I was getting ready to appear on an international talk radio program, No BS Book Club, with Sandie Sedgbeer about my book.

What unexpected events could be taking place with my work in the world? I became even more excited to see the possibilities and share with my heart. I crafted an announcement I put out over social media outlets.

Social Media Release

Hi, there! I wanted to give you a quick update on how life is moving forward for me and my business, Step Stone. It has been a summer of challenge and healing for me but I am happy to say I am now stronger and ready to start seeing more clients again. I can't tell you how happy that makes me. It is such an honor to offer the unique energy healing Spirit has gifted me with and that I get to share it with you makes my heart sing.

Starting in November I will be seeing clients on Mondays, Wednesdays and Fridays at Step Stone. I can make arrangements for Tuesday if needed. I also offer distance

Zoom sessions which can be flexible for both of us. These sessions have been amazing and, despite the distance, the energy is equally powerful.

I will be introducing some new therapies as well. I now have an Alpha Stereo Egg Chair in which we can do meditation and brain entrainment, an Oxygen Bar to boost your oxygen levels for optimum healing and a crystal bed bar that has 7 beautiful Lemurian Crystals set with lights for color therapy. Exciting things are taking place.

I also wanted to share that my bestselling books are available for purchase at the wellness center, as are essential oils, crystal water bottles, crystal pet bowls, and CBD products. With Christmas right around the corner, a unique gift that offers healing might be just the ticket. I offer gift certificates for services, too.

Oh, and one more thing, I am being interviewed for the radio program, What's Going OM? with Sandie Sedgbeer. We will be discussing my book, 20 Days Changed Everything - A Love Story Moving Through Conscious Death to Afterlife Connection, and the latest experiences I have had with my own cancer journey and healing. The show is slated to be recorded on Thursday, Oct. 28. I will make an announcement of when it will air online.

Most importantly, I hope you are doing well and I look forward to being of service to you in the near future. Sending love and blessings to you as we navigate this beautiful life together through wellness and expansion. We got this!

I knew I wanted to ask Jack if he had something he would like to share with Sandie's audience before the interview. Jack had been so close to my side all month and I just knew he would have wisdom to share. I am blessed, you are blessed, we are blessed with the ability to grow beyond our human suffering and to see the light no matter the circumstances. I was standing firmly in the light while allowing the flow of the river of life to take me.

October 21

Becki Asks Jack

Is there something you would like me to share with people in my interview with Sandie?

Jack's Response

I am pleased that you ask, my love. The energy of divine love never diminishes! NEVER! It only knows expansion, growth, and evolution. Your loved ones who have passed never lose their connection to you. Yes, we evolve, expand, have our own life journey here in the afterlife, but our love for you only grows. I encourage you to live life, love life, no matter the circumstances. We support you from here, just a small dimensional shift away, next to you; we hold you. Becki and I are learning how to navigate the subtle, and sometimes not so subtle, fields of connection and you can too. Trust is a word I am always planting in her mind and heart. I encourage you to do the same. Thank you, my love, for asking me to share. It is important for people to know our connection is real, attainable, and part of the human and soul journey. My love, trust in our love. Trust in our journey. Trust in our sharing. It is needed now more than ever.

Chapter 9
MERGING WATERS
November 2021

I WAS FEELING THE rise of a new life emerging, like a bubbling spring where the water sees the surface of the land for the first time, the wet, subterranean element feeling the kiss of sunlight as it sparkles and begins the journey across the top of the planet. I too was emerging into a new version of myself.

While gaining strength, I wrote, worked with clients, and was committed to my body, mind, and soul while I explored the meaning behind the scenes of my new-found dance with the sunlight of awareness.

Infusions became part of my regular routine and I welcomed the opportunity to honor my veins and the miraculous ability they had to carry welcome ingredients for supporting my body's natural healing. I sat in quiet contemplation as I spoke to my cells, thanked them for a job well done, and encouraged my body to remember what it felt like to have vitality, that full, expressive life-force.

I also knew heart consciousness was rising on the planet despite how it appeared on the surface. As humanity evolves, we will move into a closer connection with the compassionate energy of the universe, that of the frequency of love.

I will not say it was easy to stay in the higher state. Friends around me were getting sick with COVID while many others on the planet were leaving. It was a trying time globally and, for an energy sensitive, it was a constant vigil to maintain balance, feeling into what was mine, the other, the collective. I just knew I needed to stay open, keep my heart open to life as it was showing up without judgment, often a challenge for my thinking mind.

There are many tools to help a person gain access and maintain connection to the heart space. I constantly used focused breathing as conduit for heart connection. By placing one hand on my heart and the other on my stomach, I accessed attention to my breath. When focusing attention on my breath while feeling into my heart space, my body naturally went into a state of coherence, a level of peace that calmed my body's autonomic nervous system response, providing clearer intuitive thought.

Heart-focused meditation was another activity I used to develop a stronger connection to the faint whispers of my heart. Subtle realms are often found while relaxing into a calm state of awareness. I sought those moments. My key was to not stress about whether I was doing it right. I allowed myself to find moments to rest into my heart, regardless of how easily my mind relaxed.

In mid-November, I once again traveled to my friend Jane's cabin for some needed rest and relaxation. Our time together was always fun and, since both of us love to dance, we cranked the music and moved our bodies in ecstatic release. I could feel the beautiful, divine feminine body undulating in joy, accessing the celebration of my body moving closer and closer to my former expression, the one before losing Jack.

Jane and I were perfect partners when going into meditation, the energy between the two of us amplifying the experience for both of us. This weekend was to be no exception. Not only did we listen to a Lee Harris channeling but we tapped into a guided meditation by Lorie Ladd. I'm surprised we weren't levitating, as the energy rise was so apparent. Jack came through to me very clearly. It was as if the doorway to his realm was flung open and all I had to do was gently walk through. The walking through created a buzzing into my core and I cried tears of happiness. God was answering my prayers.

The cells vibrated with a cool energy I recognized as Jack. I felt him strongly. As the energy continued its cool vibration, I heard Spirit tell me this was the energy of healing; the cool high vibration has been used before. Regeneration of body cells took place in that field of high consciousness. I was bringing in the frequency, carrying it in my body, and then radiating it out into the world.

Jack told me he never leaves me and I felt him move into my body. He said, "We are never separate. I am never not with you. You may not always feel me but this is it. This is what we do."

I almost felt numb by the time I came out of the meditation. I was in an amazing state. I had heard Spirit repeating the phrase, "You are healing, you are healing" repeated over and over again. They said, "This cool energy is of a vibration that was known to you, Becki. It was used in other times for regeneration of the body, at the top of mountains, in cool temperatures." I understood what they were telling me. It was similar to when a spirit brushed by me and I felt a cool wash over my skin. I felt there was some significance to the cool energy of healing and high vibration that humanity is rediscovering as we evolve.

This was the ascension and I did not need to know how it would happen. I just needed to know it was happening. I did not need to know how my body was healing. I just needed to know it was healing. The amplification of energy that took place when Jane and I stepped into joy, honored life, and meditated together was validating. I truly understood the power of: *when two or more are gathered in His name.*

Hours after my time with Jane, I found my body still buzzing. I could feel Jack inside of me. My heart was blasted open with love and gratitude for the life I led, all of it. There was no mistake in any of it; my loss of Jack, my grief, my afterlife connection with him, my cancer, my COVID illness, my recovery, my remembering and claiming life here. In a state of divine rapture, I knew it was all on track. Would I have consciously chosen it? No way! But, my awareness of God, Jesus, the light of the divine, being the frequency-holder I was for that energy on the planet, coursed through my reality in a way I could neither reject nor regret. My divine mission: to step into the gentle power of that admission from the heart of my soul.

There are so many ways in which we can explore the realm of the heart, our divine center, or connection to the Creator of All That Is. If you rest into your heart then you may just find you can channel Spirit, your higher self, or free-flow write. I found the more I wrote in channel, the easier my connection seemed to stream, on and off the page.

How about trying this? Ask your heart, your higher aware-ness, a question you would like insight on. Write the question, take a deep breath, and then just write, without thought, without any predetermined set of answers. Al-low the words to flow onto the page. You may be pleasant-ly surprised at what you find written there. The more you test the waters, the easier it is to find flow of information. You bypass the thinking-mind and allow the heart-mind to play. What emerges has the potential to profoundly change your life.

I encourage you to find what works for you. The more you tap into your own unique signature, the more the subtle realm of the heart expands. As I continued to follow the internal nudge of my body, healing no longer became a maybe; it was a given. As I continued to walk into flow, synchronicity was the magic with which my day was fueled. As I continued to access my divine connection, doubt in my life path dissolved into the assuredness of the goddess I was here to be.

I never claimed to have the answers. What I did know was I would continue to strive to open to the possibilities of heart-centered action, allowing vulnerability to be a welcome companion in all aspects of my life. Choice is mine. My goal became to live expanded compassion, calling on the support of God, Jesus, Mother Mary, Mary Magdalene, my guides, my higher soul connection, and my beloved Jack.

I learned to accept Jack as an extension of the divine love we shared. No matter what life would bring for me to experience while on this Earth plane, I welcomed it with open arms, ready to face the dark nights as well as turn my eyes to the beautiful bright days this messy human life offers.

Thanksgiving held a deeper meaning for me than at any other time in my life. I stood in grateful joy with respect to all I had experienced, learned, witnessed, recognized, and conquered. I felt a new version of Becki emerging from the deep waters of life as I kept allowing the waters to flow. I wondered what Jack had to share.

Jack Responds to Becki

Yes, you feel me. Of course you do. The more you walk as one with me, the more your channeling becomes a natural state of being. It feels so natural to you, you think I am not around. Feel me smile, for the more linear time you experience, the more it will feel like I am not here; yet I am so at one with you, I am you and you are me, the beautiful blending of our souls as we have done for eons. It is from that place of coupling we get to share with the world. Our journey was absolutely what it was supposed to be and your survival through the roughest time of your life part of the fuel to ignite your recovery. You are the one to ignite others, my love, but I will be within you fanning the flame of love, of divine compassion, of the light in form you get to serve to others. Bask in your new-found strength of Spirit. Use whatever words take you to power within for it is from within your heart I dwell. It is within your heart that God shines his grace upon you. You have been given the gift of physical life, my love. Let me imbue you with the everlasting bond we share.

Chapter 10
WATERS EBB AND FLOW
December 2021

"Remember the magic, my love. The more you remember the magic and step into joy, the more your body heals and I know you feel it happening. Dance, laugh, love. When you do, I am there infusing you with light to amplify your soul."
Jack

DECEMBER ROLLED IN WITH a calm countenance, ushering in a month of gratitude with the ebb and flow of life. Perhaps death's door has a way of bringing a person to their knees in prayer, into gazing at the gentle flicker of the everlasting flame of the soul in a way that transcends the mundane. It was as if everything I looked at carried a mystical quality, a magical expression, and I was at center stage for the show.

There are times when the mystical takes on the quality of reality and the lines of dimensional fields become blurred. One night, in the early morning hours while I was lying in bed in a half-awake and half-asleep state, I dreamt of Jack. I was not completely asleep but in the in-between state of awareness. I was in bed with my arms around Jack, spooning him from behind, feeling the mass of his body under my arm as I cuddled him tenderly. I literally felt him but then thought, "How can this be you, Jack? How can it be that I am actually feeling your body when you are no longer here?" I was confused. My mind tried to reason what was happening and at the same time relish the moment, make it last. I was in-between realms and I wanted to stay there. Then, Jack got up out of bed as if to go make coffee. He had brought me coffee in bed every morning while we were together. At the doorway, he turned toward me and smiled, then walked away. He did not return with coffee and I gently wept for the beauty of the gift he had given me that morning. I knew he had visited.

Despite the challenge of moving on in life without Jack, I navigated the challenge with courage and fortitude for a life ahead. I knew I was here to live life beyond unwellness, that love would find me again, and that Jack was forever a part of my soul essence.

I continued to have twice-weekly infusions which helped my life force energy feel robust and vigorous. As a way of appreciating my journey and reaching out in service to other people, I decided to make video recordings while my body took in life-enhancing elixir.

Becki Video Recording December 8

Another day, another infusion. Life is so worth living, moment to precious moment, regardless of what the outside circumstances seem to be. There is not a person on the planet who does not have something challenging to deal with, whether it is personal, physical, with a loved one, or outside circumstance. Regardless, finding the ability to move into a state of gratitude is a choice we have in every now moment. Can we work towards a greater life full of love and support the resiliency of the human heart? I, for one, will send out love to everyone, support to everyone, big hugs and lots of light.

I recorded these words while sitting in a chair, hooked up to an IV bag, receiving an infusion of vitamins and anti-cancer support. I took those precious moments to walk with grace and humility to the wonderful care being given to me by my naturopathic team, family, and friends. Many people were walking with me through the ebb and flow of a more empowered life.

December 13

Becki Video Recording

Another day, another infusion, sitting here, passing the time. Again, I am stepping into gratitude. It is so important to find gratitude even amidst some of the challenges we face. It lightens the spirit when you can find something to be grateful for, life, breath... Breathe. I am sitting here breathing. All is good in this moment, in this now. I just need to remember that. If I could share anything in this process of healing, the healing journey I am on, it would be to find gratitude. It hasn't been easy. It is not easy to have cancer and to go through what the body experiences. The challenges you walk through: weight loss, hair loss, lack of wellness. If you look at me, it doesn't look like I have lost hair but luckily my hair was thick to begin with. The reality is that I am losing it. I had to go to that place of realizing it is just hair. If it all goes away, it is okay because I am still here, I am still breathing. There are other things that are more important. So, breathing the breath of life, I take in some nutrients and some supplements that are healthy for my body as I continue to explore this amazing connection to being human, being in this human body. Witnessing the amazing light-being, the amazing soul in this physicality, right now, as a human experiencing living on this planet. I am ever so grateful to be in this body doing what I am doing, sharing, living, loving, being here; able to be in service to all people, in some way, in some fashion. Sending love out to everyone, the most important thing being love. I love my life, I love you. I love my family and friends. I have so much to be grateful for. I love my connection to God and Jesus and all the ascended masters, the angels, my guides, Jack, my spiritual connections, and my connections in this life. Take care everyone. Please take care. Breathe into the moment. Okay? Love you. Bye for now.

This month's bloodwork showed a significant drop in the cancer markers. The proof was in the pudding. The actions I had been taking showed a drop into "well within normal range" in a very short period of time, the higher breast cancer marker continuing to rapidly reduce. For me, it was a validation that following my intuition was right on track. My flow was towards health. I was re-

bounding in life force energy and my physical body clearly revealed the results of all the dedicated effort taking
place. I approached the Christmas holiday with such hope
and promise for a bright future, the gift of the season was
mine. My humble prayers were answered.

Facing your own mortality often changes you. I suspect
my connection to the divinity within me was a catalyst
for deepening my awareness of God and Jesus in my life.
My healing journey did not exist in isolated components
of body, mind, spirit; all aspects were working as one
unit, one vibrational divine essence. I had never doubted
the power of the sacred and divine connection I always
had but somehow, the reality of divinity guiding my life
became more real, tangible. I was witnessing the result
of an active participation with the power of light, the
consciousness of all-encompassing compassionate love.
Christmas took on a glow unlike any before.

Out of the glowing light, I was contacted by a dear friend
and mentor, Lee Harris. We have known each other for
many years and he knew I had written a book about
my journey with Jack during and after his passage. Lee
was inviting me to be interviewed on his show Impact
The World Podcast, a free offering where he interviews
change makers and entrepreneurs whose work changes
lives. He was hoping I would be interested in being a
guest. This gift was an undeniable opportunity to share
with the world the journey Jack and I took. And, to have
the man who had had such an impact on my life inter-

viewing me was an answer to prayers I didn't even know I had.

I was ready to move forward in all aspects; life, love, business, personal happiness, and spiritual expansion. At this point, no matter what life dealt me, I knew it was part of a divine offering and I knew Jack was by my side, cheering me on all along the way.

Jack's Response to Becki

"I am so full of love for you, Becki. I am always encouraging you to find your way, walk in beauty and full awareness of the sacred path you have walked. What is shifting is your recognition of the unfolding of divine timing and the honoring of your life in ways you never dreamed. From my vantage, the expansion of love is never-ending. It is an energetic frequency becoming more and more available to humans as ascension continues on the spectrum of evolution. You, my love, are a shining example of the human potential to rise above and claim life, claim love, claim joy. There must be those who can carry the torch for others, the wayshowers. Thank you for lighting the way to relationship with the sacred, the energy of the beloved, the possibility of continued connection to those in the afterlife. Your connection to me has been a huge factor in healing your body; your cells are able to access the frequency of wellness through a high vibrational state. Keep it up, my love. You are not leaving me; you are moving forward in life. It is as it is supposed to be. That is the gift.

Chapter 11

FILLING THE VESSELS

January 2022

"The ability of the human body to experience divine love is coming onto the planet in waves of light. You will be teaching others how to navigate these waves of love, all forms of love. You can do this; I am right here with you. I love you madly." Jack

ELATION FILLED MY BODY while my breath was visible in the frigid night air. The wind cut through my coat with a chill I felt down to my bones but I was high on life. I stood with my mom in the street as fireworks exploded overhead. We were ringing in the New Year on Fremont Street in Las Vegas, Nevada. We had joined my cousin and her friend for a night of celebration, danced to the numerous bands that lined the street, watched the spectacular light show overhead, and took in the sights and sounds of thousands of people in their unique human expressions, celebrating in their own way.

The new year held great promise for me. I knew 2022 would be a more productive, life-enhancing year and I was ready to step into Becki in a way like never before. My defenses were down. New courage was pulsing through my veins and on top of all of that, I was ready to experience joy, the kind of joy available to us by choice. I knew I could choose, at any moment in time, how I would view my reality. Had not the envelope of paradigms been ripped open and exposed? The Supergirl in me anticipated the year with a Bring It On attitude.

Unbeknownst to me, that night, I ended up with direct exposure to COVID again. The miraculous thing was, I did not get sick. I did my due diligence not to expose anyone else but several days later found me strong and no worse for wear. I was confident in my body and my immune system coming on board again. It wasn't about reckless abandon with my health but it was an honoring of the power my body had to do the job it was designed to do, heal. I knew from the depths of my core that healing was my natural state of being.

Back in Montana, clients were coming in through the door and I had this feeling of anticipation. I was not exactly sure why, but I could feel an energy building in me. Was it with my work? Was it with my heath? Was it that I would meet someone special? It did not matter. The energy of life evolving was making itself known.

I had a reading with the LightKeepers in mid-January which validated much of the excitement I was feeling. Jack was very present and reminded me I was not moving on from him but I was going forward. He was excited for me. He wanted me to go forward in life. The Light-

Keepers said there was going to be a second book related to my healing journey and perhaps third book related to being open to love after loss. They said I would find love, a different love than Jack but a new love nonetheless. The theme for the year of 2022 for me was patience, compassion, and gratitude. I would find those energies within everything I did. Jack would help me move into mediumship in a trusting and natural way. It would come with ease and joy. The LightKeepers suggested I play with the energies; let it happen. "When you do your best, God does the rest," was the mantra of the day.

The more I let go and got out of my own way, the easier it was to fill my energetic vessels with light, love, compassion, and acceptance. I vowed to do my best, to the best of my ability. I committed to holding the hand of the divine with every human step and, if I tripped and fell, I would get up and keep stepping.

A beautiful, heart-centered woman contacted me to be interviewed on another social media platform for widows, women who had lost their loved ones and were seeking tools to help them along the way. It was an honor to share with these women, to hold space for their questions, to be in service to their grief in a way that could give them hope. My world was expanding and I could feel the wave of energy building behind me.

One day I went into channel and asked, "What does my higher self want to share with me today?" The answer was simple, "LOVE. Love is the key to all connection."

I was connecting from my vulnerable, open, raw heart and my guidance kept pointing the compass to those connections and opportunities being presented as if a door had opened into a magical world of love in all forms. I lived and breathed the deep waters of love and felt ready to shout it out to anyone who wanted to hear.

Infusions became my friend. Supporting my body with good food, healthy supplements, rest, and fun was a priority.

Jack's birthday was on the horizon. I had been working with him in so many different ways, opening the door to our expanded soul infusion, ever evolving, and yet I knew the day would hold memories, energies that might not all be easy. The vastness of heart emotions can lead to getting lost sometimes in the feeling of those emotions. The month's time flew by and the next thing I knew, it was the 23rd.

January 23

Becki to Jack

Happy birthday, my love. You have been in my heart all day. I danced for you, connected in meditation and Reiki. Your friend Jozy was here and many sent their love to you! Funny, I know you already know all of this but it feels good for me to write it down, somehow making the day with you seem more tangible, real to my physical body. Do you have anything you would like to share with me?

Jack's Words to Becki

Yes! Breathe my love, just breathe. That's it. Feel me going into your lungs, my love embracing your heart through breath. I have been with you all day. It was nice to have Jozy here, the prodigal warrior. Be aware and stay focused, my love. You can get pulled into a life that could be fun but not all yours. You will find balance. Keep putting effort into connecting with me, writing, and sharing. You have a big year coming and you will need self-care to be a huge part of your daily routine. Hydrate. Water, water, water, water! Go get some now!

I took Jack's advice, stopped channel writing to take a side journey for some water before returning to writing. I smiled at the fact he was still taking care of me from his realm even if he could not physically fetch me the water.

Jack's Words to Becki

I am doing amazing things, my love. Part of the evolution I'm going through and an aspect I will be bringing through to you as we continue to be one with each other. Becki, I love you and I will always be here. You have much to do and I will always be by your side, your wing man patrolling the perimeter of your etheric field. You can feel safe with me as your guardian. You are not moving away from me and, if anything, this year will find us in relationship in a whole new, more expanded way as we explore the divine love connection we have shared for eons. You and I, many lives together, many experiences of love, growth, and expansion. Hold onto that awareness and develop the management of those frequencies. You are grounding that energy and it is so important now. The ability for the human body to experience divine love is coming onto the planet in waves of light. You will be teaching others how to navigate these waves of love, all forms of love. You can do this; I am right here with you. I love you madly.

Becki's Voice Recorded Message to Jack at Bedtime

It's January 23, the end of the day on your birthday, Jack. You're 67, Jack. Gosh, 67! At least in linear Earth terms this time around. I had a really, really good day remembering you. Having you come into meditation with me this morning, feeling you, dancing for you, honoring you, sharing your birthday with others. Listening to songs dedicated to you, Pink Floyd, just remembering us. It was good to see Jozy again. It has been a while. He is all excited to be connecting again. I wanted to get on and record because I was just doing channel writing with you and I remembered how we used to do this together; we would talk about how much we loved each other.

We would try to outdo one another in how we spoke. For example; I would say, I love you beyond the universe, beyond time and space, beyond the beyond. And then you would say, I love you even more than that. Or I would come up with another way to say it and then you would come back with something and we would go back and forth talking about how we loved each other three-madly (I love you madly, madly, madly). I love you more than the stars in the sky, bigger than all the universes combined. Oh Jack, I so miss that. We were so well suited; we are so suited. I shouldn't *talk about you in the past. I just miss you being here. There are times when I miss your physical presence because we were so suited for one another in this life.*

Oh, Jack! Okay, I know. This afterlife connection is what we get to do. Oh dang, this is what we get to do. I'm going to be talking to Lee Harris soon and sharing with others. I have to start writing again. I know you keep encouraging me to write. My love, I want to feel you, I want to feel you tonight. Okay? I'm going to put this phone down, I'm going to turn the lights out, and I'm going to the place we meet. Jack, I love you! Happy Birthday!

Chapter 12

WATERFALL INTO ABUNDANCE

February 2021

"Remember to breathe it all in my love, every exquisite experience. Life continues to unfold in an ever-changing dance of divine light and love and you, Becki, are ready to embrace what is yours. Accept it in honor of you." Jack

I FOUND MYSELF BREATHING into life in a way that naturally produced a self-generating field of energy supporting healing through all aspects of life; physical, mental, emotional, and spiritual. These realms were all part of the wholeness of who Becki was, who I was evolving into, who I was manifesting into on a moment-to-moment basis. Hope for a bright future was the ever-evolving target I was striving to hit. Often, I found my mark but I also recognized my human emotions and the fragility life can sometimes be.

Jack had been encouraging me to move forward in life, to find love, to live to my fullest. I was grateful for his encouragement because truly, it was the greatest challenge I faced, well outside of my own walk on death's tight rope. But even death's tightrope felt like a wide bridge I had navigated with courage and grace compared to the daunting idea of my life going forward without the physical love and presence of Jack. The messy, emotional aspects of my journey forward was a constant letting go, again and again. Yet, when I remembered to breathe into the light of God, walk hand-in-hand with Jesus while holding my new-found life force, I knew abundance would be mine, love was all that existed, and Jack was forever by my side.

I had always been blessed with the ability to laugh easily. When my roommate, Jane and I got into conversations, we often found ourselves laughing so hard we were crying, doubled over grabbing our bellies in complete surrender to the moment. Laughter is an energy of elevation taking you into higher dimensions. It was so much easier for me to go into bliss states of awareness while laughing and joking around. It was healing to my soul, my heart lightened, and I felt my body move into waves of release, stress and tension leaving my muscles. Jane and I had recorded short video conversations on our Youtube channel, Cosmic Conversations with Becki and Jane, and invariably, we ended up laughing while sharing our simple life adventures. I would go back and watch our episodes, especially the ones where laughter overtook us and invariably, I would join in the laughter as it was so dang contagious. It was another form of healing that seemed to be working to my advantage.

My latest blood tests showed a continual drop in cancer markers; I was well within normal range. The actions I continued to take were showing results in a physical, tangible way even though many of those actions were taking place in the quantum field. Energy healing was such a huge part of my everyday protocol. I stepped into a knowing, the kind of awareness leading to a solid foundation for building a sound structure to house a whole new Becki, so the trickling waters of life could come together bit-by-bit to form the beautiful waterfall just waiting to be viewed in awe.

I wanted to talk to everyone I encountered. The light within could not be contained and I was shining for all to see. I knew the light within was healing me but would this light attract new relationships into my life? Would this light help me bring my business to a new level of support, not only for me but for the people I served?

In life, Jack had the insight I held myself back while I was with him. He knew our love was so strong, so all encompassing, I would choose to spend my energy hanging out with him, whiling the hours away in his energy field, talking the hours away in a no-time, time warp. During his dying process, he shared with me that he knew I would shine brightly; I would find success in life in a way I could not do with him in here. He often said he held me back from flying forward in my business, despite my protests to the contrary. The truth is he was right. When I had a choice to put energy into my business or just hang out with him, I chose him every time and we would get lost in the energy of the moment. While in complete honor of what Jack and I shared, I recognized the bigger service I always felt I was here to do was unfolding: to write, to share, to be open and vulnerable to my humanity so I could help someone else. I was birthing into a much bigger and broader version of myself, the pieces of me gathering momentum drop-by-drop as the life force volume continued to build momentum.

One of the ways this expansion took place was in my connection to Lee Harris. He is an amazing soul on this planet and I had mentored with him for ten years. His work was a foundational piece in my comfort level to step into energy healing and channeling. Lee and his team produce a podcast show called Impact the World. He had contacted me in December to see if I would consider being a guest on his show. I gladly accepted and our interview took place preparing for a show release in March.

Lee helped me feel at ease and, of course, Jack was there laughing and encouraging the conversation. What a treat for me to be in Lee's presence discussing our book, *20 Days Changed Everything*. The door opened for me to also discuss my cancer journey. I was being gifted the opportunity to enter a global community in a way I could never have made happen on my own. I could hear Jack saying, "See, my love, you are soaring and shining so bright. Step into your life. Your sharing will help so many people."

It was as if my life force energy was a spring runoff, building on itself to then cascade like the waterfall into a bottomless pool of sacred and abundant energy. What did that mean to my body? It meant my physical body continued to improve in vitality, my mood elevated. I felt hope for my future and I shared the love of being in service with my family, friends, and clients.

Dancing was on the agenda often. My spirits always elevated when listening and moving my body in rhythm to music. I placed my hands on my body, gently feeling my hands move across the surface of my clothes as I swayed with my eyes closed. I thought about how amazing my body was, how miraculous healing can take place, how I was designed for healing, balance, and embracing life. I would feel my cells start to vibrate, sometimes chills would run up and down my spine as confirmation in the moment.

But it was so much more than my healing. I knew I had been given a gift from God. My journey was to understand the bigger picture to my awareness, the gift of my profession as an energy intuitive, the communication of a compassionate love for all with whom I come in contact. My job was to continue to translate the knowing that was bestowed upon me. The interview with Lee would be one such avenue to the next level of living I was being called to welcome.

Boots-on-the-ground efforts were made to up-level my business in order to accommodate a much more global audience. I worked at stepping out of fear into a boldness borne of a mission to help others. If I could find my way to my own voice, others could too. If I navigated the deep waters of loss and grief, others did too. If I found my way through the valley of death by using my own internal body compass, then someone else might discover their internal compass as well. I knew I could be a cheerleader for other people navigating the tumultuous waters of their physical and emotional landscape. I would hold space for them to find the way to their internal divinity. I found myself understanding Jesus and Mary Magdalene in a profoundly intimate way, feeling the love of people pulsing through my veins, in reverence to the human experience. Life became a walking, breathing prayer to the divine within all.

Jack was right all along; I was ready to soar and he was my wingman.

Jack's Message

"Here you are, my love, walking into a life that can feel intense yet you are handling it with grace. Remember that life here and there is in perpetual motion, part of an unending cycle of expansion and growth. I am exploring the waves of vibration where they lead me, furthering the growth I am honored to experience. We are both growing beyond our individual connection to a more expanded and all-encompassing absorption into the field of cosmic light, the oneness of all that is. Thank you for embracing your life, my love, despite the pain of your loss of me, the challenge of your health, the uncertainty of your future. For it is in your breathing through it all that you will find our love, your divinity, your living life forward. Humans are at a crossroads, many seeking the signs to show them the way back home to themselves, the God within. Life is magic

and you, my love, are in a unique position to point to the signs those who find you are looking for. Embrace your life like you never have before. Let the cascading waterfall shower you with abundance in all forms. You are loved three madly!"

Chapter 13

SURFING THE CREST OF THE WAVE

March 2022

"I am forever near, not separate from but a part of the flavor of your life. Taste the beauty of this divine love we share. The scrumptious delicacy of energetic intimacy is ours, my love." Jack

"PHYSICAL ATTRACTION IS COMMON, *but Cosmic connection is rare,"* according to a FaceBook post on Dolores Cannon's page. I was blessed to experience this connection with my beloved, Jack. While I remained connected to him in his divine afterlife form, I was infused with the cosmic energy of love he shared with me, through me. I was learning to carry and hold a frequency of energy that could not be described adequately with words but was felt from the very core of my being. I was striving to share that energy with others as that energy is a frequency to be experienced in the body, in service to God, the divine within and without.

I was asked by a client, "What is it you did to keep your physical body here? What did you do where the rubber meets the road?" In other words, what tangible activities did I do to keep going down the road to recovery from all I had experienced since Jack's transition into Spirit? While I mention different activities throughout the months following his passage and leading into and through my own cancer, the biggest piece for me was connection to Spirit, finding my soul journey through the grace of God, the divine. I recognized that not everyone shared the awareness of Spirit in the same way I did but I knew I could take their hand into the fields of energy healing, opening portals for them to begin to experience the esoteric side of their lives. By being open to sharing aspects of my private life in a very public way, I knew some people may find comfort.

March 6, 2022

Becki's Social Media Post

It has been a while since I have shared personal thoughts in a public way. But this morning I feel compelled to be vulnerable, open, speaking my truth. Despite the great heartache of loss of my beloved Jack 2 1/2 years ago, I experience afterlife connection with him and channel his messages. He came to me this morning and these were his words of comfort...

Jack's Message to Becki

"Let me hold you, feel me, breathe me. I am forever near, not separate from but a part of the flavor of your life. Taste the beauty of this divine love we share. The scrumptious

delicacy of energetic intimacy is ours, my love. Allow this blessed love energy to infiltrate your body, your cells, your soul. We are one." Jack

There is so much grief, so much loss and yet, can we learn to turn our eyes to awareness of the divine, the higher purpose, the subtle energies of light and love that are swirling around us always? It is not about diminishing anyone's experience of life but embracing it all as we embody this Earth suit, navigating life while remembering our divinity.

While Jack holds me in an energetic embrace, let me hold space for you, let me send you love, let me be of service to the hearts that need held right now.

May you find peace. May you find solace. May you find compassion. May you find love today.

I'd been contemplating the whole idea of a divine love, the divine connection I experienced with Jack now being in the other realm, that higher awareness, higher dimensional realm. What did it mean to connect with the kind of vibration that shakes you to the core? Where every cell in your body seems to be on high alert, vibrating with an essence of a love that there really are no words to do it justice.

I experienced that in a Reiki session one day in early March, 2022. I was on the table and Diana was giving me Reiki. When she placed her hands to my heart space, I saw myself standing in my heart. The heart itself was a lotus flower. The lotus started out a light pink and then transformed, getting a little bit darker in color. While I was standing in this beautiful and delicate flower, flames started to move up and around my body. My body was being engulfed in this beautiful light-purple flame. The flame was calming, loving; it filled my soul with complete joy and elation. As I stood in the flame in the lotus, Jack approached me and stepped inside the lotus flower with me. We embraced. As we embraced, my state of being moved to bliss and I felt every cell in my body vibrating with a love, an intensity that was hard to contain. And yet, it felt completely natural, as if this was my most natural state of being. Jack and my energies blended into one essence and this essence was planted inside my heart, the beautiful lotus flower that symbolized this love, this beautiful, gentle love. As our energies swirled, I felt alive, full of light, full of potential. The love I felt within me and without was Christ consciousness, the love of the divine beloved. It is an energy we, as humans, have the potential to feel, to know, and to experience with the wholeness of our being. It is what I experienced when my body felt the vibration, the frequency of that love. Let me explain.

Every cell in my body would start to tingle, sort of like when you get the chills, or an energy runs up the back of your neck. Only instead of it being in one place, I felt the tingling in my whole body; my feet were vibrating, my legs vibrating, my hands and arms vibrating, I felt it in my stomach, my heart, my chest, breathing deeply feeling the energies rise. My head would start to tingle as if someone was tickling my hair. My root chakra area would start to tingle. My sacral chakra, my uterus area, would all start to feel energy. The kundalini energy wave started to rise from my root chakra to my crown chakra. It felt as if every cell in my body was vibrating. As the vibration continued, I felt the rise of energy and the sensation was very sensual. My heart expanded. Tears began to flow from my eyes. Sometimes my arms literally began to shake.

As I allowed the energies to flow, the frequency rose, taking me into a bliss state of being. I often connected with Jack and could feel him enter my body. It was as if his energetic field entered my root chakra and I began pulsating. I would feel his energy as a cool, fresh wash enter me. That's how I knew it was him: I felt the coolness of his energy whenever he was near. There was a power from the energy I felt from Jack when he was inside of me that way. The energetic rise into an orgasmic experience was breathtaking, a different type of orgasm than from a physical manipulation. It was my body's response to an energetic field or frequency I never knew was possible until I experienced it with Jack. The beauty of being able to connect with him that way was beyond imagination. The subtle realm of energy was what I learned to dance with. It was an energy Jack encouraged me to learn to work with, to hold, to feel, to move, and to experience. The kind of love my soul was being absorbed in and held in was a higher-level frequency I was learning to adapt and hold within me. It was the very thing Jack explained we are here to do. His connection with me in that vibrational frequency of the Divine love of the beloved, coupled with my ability to absorb the frequency and hold it within my body, was the learning and then the teaching we were to do together.

I knew I was healing when my cells were vibrating in that frequency. Not only was I healing myself, but I held the frequency of healing within my energetic field, which then impacted those around me. In my auric field resided a divine connection to the Christ consciousness of love. I felt the power of that holding. I felt the magnitude of carrying the capacity to love beyond the human experience. I felt humbled and honored that Jack and I continued to work in this capacity, sharing this kind of never-ending love with the world. And I got to heal my own body, my own pain and suffering, my own physical challenge, by being in the energy he helped me hold. I found myself navigating new territory in relationships on the physical plane. I recognized that by holding the love frequency in the energy work I did, it could be misunderstood. And yet, holding space for another human to experience the energy of that love, to hold them in the vibration of that love, was a responsibility I was willing to take on. I recognized my journey with Jack was this, the now I shared with him. I would not have experienced the divine blessed beingness I experienced now if he were still here on the planet. I honored the journey. I honored my navigation of a new life without him here physically yet very much present in my reality, very much present in my work, very much present as a part of my soul.

Another Level I & II Reiki Training was scheduled and I was looking forward to where the weekend would take all who participated. What kind of magic would weave its way into being this time?

March 19, 2022

Journal Entry for Reiki Level I & II

Holy Ocean of Love meditation

Walking down the path, Jack was with me and so was a dear male friend of mine when I felt the energy of a third man enter my awareness: the men in my life from the last few days. I felt confused as I just wanted it to be Jack. He encouraged me to keep walking forward on the path, regardless of my confusion. He told me I would understand. I came to the log and sat down by myself gazing at the ocean. I felt the purple flame of Saint Germain engulf me with peace and saw the ocean waves rising and falling in front of me. I watched the waves. Jack shared I was learning, navigating all aspects of love just like the crest and crash of the waves. I would feel the bliss of the top of the wave but also needed to be aware of the crashing of the waves. It was all part of the experience and aspects we would be writing about in our book. It was all OK, he assured me. You are navigating beautifully, Becki. Become one with the waves so the crashing does not hurt so much but becomes part of the energy exchange. Then I went into snippets of awareness, feeling into the ebb and flow of the water. I felt Jack's cool energy enter my body.

March 19, 2022

Journal Entry for Reiki Level I & II

Reiki Placement

I was walking in a beautiful redwood forest and came to a clearing where the grass was blowing in a warm breeze. As I walked, the high grasses swayed under my hands. It was gentle, warm, beautiful, my soul was full of joy. I lay down and peered up through the grass into the sky. I saw Jack's hand come down through the light, the clouds, and he beckoned me to join him. I felt his deep and abiding love flow into my body. My whole body tingled with love, light, and vibration. I gladly joined him as he went into the light, into the heavens. We were greeted by angels, guides, beings of light and, as we passed by them, they bowed in reverence. Jack said to me how honored I was for the journey I took, continued to take. The depth of awareness into the task of holding this divine love and sharing was huge. They then took me to a room where I was bathed in the purple flame and my being began to glow. Jack repeated the words, "You are special. You are always going to be special. You are this bright light. Don't let anyone dim your light. Hold firm in the journey, Becki. Feel the frequency being radiated in your body. Hold that frequency, my love."

March 20, 2022

Journal Entry for Reiki Level I & II

River of Holy Fire

The forest was magical. Redwoods majestic, the pathway strewn with moss, needles, and flowers. The smell of the trees and plants was infiltrating into my body. Jack was present, playful, joyful. He told me to relax and enjoy. This is a lighthearted journey. We walked with Gaia, the Earth Mother. It was food for my soul and the connection was strong. We walked the path along the river, having fun. Jack reminded me to notice the small things. "Take awe in the beauty surrounding you, Becki." We came to the bend in the river and the water was shimmering like liquid gold as we walked into it. Mary Magdalene was there at the bank and walked in with us. Jesus was there too. They took me in and were bathing me in the liquid gold of the water. I reminded them they had already baptized me in the ocean water. They smiled and Jesus said, "You can always be born anew. The water is a symbol of cleansing love. Allow it to flow through you, to infiltrate your very being. Like the water cycle of Earth, love has many forms so honor all forms. Water and love are powerful forces. Allow both to move. Then we walked to the beach and I lay down on the warm ground. Jack was at my head, Jesus to my left, Mary to my right, and my guide Micha at my feet. They were healing me, grounding me, reminding me to just be. My body became very warm as I allowed, received. My mind wandered and I became aware my life was all okay. They said to me, "Enjoy the healing energy and let flow happen." I needed a light heart today.

Becki Writes to Jack

This thing we do, Jack, this love we share that transcends any human emotion, that bridges the human and the divine, this is what we do, my love. As I step into the depths of writing our book, I'm learning to understand the energy of sacred love in a way I've never experienced before. I *understand now when you say you're always with me, a part of the essence of my soul. You always come through, taking care of me, helping guide me, dressing my wounds. Oh God, how is it possible to move on in love when I know divine love, the love that knows no bounds? And yet, the physical body, the human aspect of Becki who is grounded here on the planet, wants to be held, caressed, to experience making love, being loved by a man in body. I want to experience the passion of a man touching my skin, feeling the electrical charges move through my body in a way that can only happen through physical touch. I am in a unique position to experience the sacred love of my beloved and the physical love of a man here on the planet still in a body with me. I am blessed beyond measure, to know I'm being held in all dimensions of reality, I am being loved in all dimensions of reality, I have been gifted life and a birthing into a new version of myself. God, may I walk the life you see for me? Jack, may I stay true to the love connection we share, that we have always shared, in the divinity of us? To my new Love, may I grow with you in this life and the physical enjoying of what this life has to offer us?*

The events of the month had prepared me for the broadcast of my interview with Lee Harris on Impact the World. There was no turning back. The sharing of the journey was to be part of my destiny, an expansion of living life fully and openly in the world without apology. Becki was living life forward!

Chapter 14

CONCLUSION

I T IS AN HONOR for me at this stage in my life to be embarking on this journey to self, because from this internal journey, I have found my passion and my calling which includes reaching out into the world in a much bigger way, using a much broader brush stroke. I am at my most comfortable place within when I am sharing life from the heart, from love filled with compassion. It is in the sharing that I heal, learn, and grow. Even as I share my own life experiences, I expand into a fuller version of myself through listening, being a light for others, absorbing others' stories and experiences. We as humans are much more "alike" than we often realize. When we go to that vulnerable place, that place inside of us only we know about, the deep and hidden aspects of ourselves we tend to hide from the rest of the world, it is then when we are most alike. It is from that place of "humanness" we can connect, creating huge and lasting impact, if we just allow. Even though it may feel like we're all alone in the world, that no one understands us, it is from that deep and tender place called the heart that we truly unite. We are one when we enter the field of the heart, the field of love. When we're in that field of the heart, there is no color, gender, difference; we are all beautifully human. So it is from that place I choose to journey and express in the world. I offer my own life experience so you will know you are not alone! I offer up my vulnerability so we can all evolve together into a much more compassionate world.

July 27, 2022

Jack's Message to Becki

"You're not forgotten, my love. You are a conduit for connection, voice to the amazing love we share, the beautiful divinity of energy filtered through your body and brought to Earth in the way we know and understand. We have done this many times. Don't doubt that. You are still growing into your essence, your light, your divine power, and you must stabilize those energies as they are more powerful than you are used to. That is why the diversion of relationship has been good for you. You needed this time to walk gently towards these moments, the work you are here to do for us, for others, for you, your soul. We are but one aspect of the multi-layered nature of this life experience through your body. You are feeling stronger physically and I am grateful to your friend for helping you find that strength, a different version of love. Allow it to be, my love. Your friend does not possess the awareness you do when it relates to energy and yet he has a beautiful heart. That is the draw for you. You connect to his tenderness, his soul essence that is love. Allow yourself to continue to be open. Your friend will help you as you are helping him. It is OK to be patient. You have your own life to live. We have a book to write, my love. I *am not leaving. This is our chosen path. I have much to share and the writing will be a stronger and stronger urge as you know the timeline. I do love the title you came up with and the chapters will flow once you step back into the energy of writing. See how easy your pen is flowing now, the words flying out faster than your pen can move. Soon, you will feel comfortable speaking these channels into the phone recorder. The book will flow from your heart once you step out of your own way.*

I love you, Becki. I am not leaving you alone. You have me. You have always had me. I am not far. And I was so happy you connected with the psychic the other day because I wanted you to know we can still be together here, in the physical, an aspect of my coming back in to be with you. We have been gifted this opportunity, my love, because of the work we do, the people we will help, the people we already helped, past, present, and future, all at one with the energy we carry. Can you accept the fact that you carry great healing? Can you accept the fact that we are needed, we carry an energy that is shifting Earth and humanity? Can you allow for the awareness that you are a powerful soul, my love, and it had to be you, through your body that the transmissions had to happen? Can you truly understand the beauty of your soul, the strength it took for you to say yes? You have been preparing for so many lifetimes to be in this now, standing in the light of true and abiding love and then sharing it with the world. I could not have done what you do, my love. You were the one. Do you truly understand the sacred and everlasting love I have for you? Can you accept that the Angels sing for you? Can you allow your tears of truth to flow as you feel the love of God? You are known, my love, and it is not about ego. It is about you understanding the depths of your divine connection. You walk the path of one devoted to the light, to the compassionate love of Christ, the Christed one, with the devotion of one such as Mary Magdalene. You are beginning to understand the guidance you are receiving to write such a book. Allow the tears of awareness to open you up to all possibilities. You are so loved."

Becki asks, "Jack, who am I?"

"You are an angel, my love. Others see that in you. Honor who you are! I will be here to support you all along the way. You are never alone, my love. I know you miss me, which is why we have been gifted the opportunity for an aspect of me to come to you. God is gifting you, me, us. Step in to that sacred love, Becki. It is the frequency you were born to reside. Do not be in fear of it. Let it flow freely from you like the tears you are shedding now. Feel your heart, feel everything. It is all part of the sharing. Grab hold of life, my love. Grab hold of me. Grab hold of God. You walk the path of light. You are the beacon for so many souls. Teach others to breathe the deep waters of love."

Every breath I take, every tear I cry, every challenge I have faced were all part of the beauty of this human body my soul chose to walk with. Gratitude was ever present and I have often said, "I will love life through this body for as long as I am here, each precious moment. I will honor my body, my cells, my body's innate wisdom, and will listen to the best of my ability to what it shares."

Thank you for taking the journey with me. You know me and some part of me knows you, as we are all connected in the field of our humanity through heart-centered awareness and love. We share a common human experience together and when we join our hearts, the oneness of life flows into our breath, allowing us to dive deep into the chambers of the heart, compassion, and love ever-flowing. If I can do this life, live and grow, so can YOU! We, as divine humans, are designed to be able to Breathe The Deep Waters Of Love, all versions and expressions of love. As long as there is breath.........

RESOURCES

I was honored with assistance from the people and organizations in this list. Others I worked with are not listed but receive my heartfelt gratitude and loving support.

Lee Harris, Intuitive Guide, Transformation Teacher, Musician

https://leeharrisenergy.com

Sandie Sedgbeer, Journalist, Author, Talk TV & Radio Sho Host, Editor

https://sedgbeer.com

Lorie Ladd, Ascension Teacher, Multidimensional Channel

https://lorieladd.com

Barbara Rose, Spiritual Energy Healer, Hypnotherapist, Minister, Channeler, Medium

https://sparksofthedivine.com

Hillary Sargent, Two Poppies Apothecary, Nutritional Herbalist, Bioresonance, BodyTalk

https://twopoppiesapothecary.com

Diana Schmeling, Holy Fire III Karuna Master, Craniosacral Therapy, Wisdom Keeper

https://heartsongtlc.com

Inge Peterson, Holy Fire III Karuna Master, Body Talk, Zilis CBD Nutritional

Https://yourbestlifemt.com

Sarah Jane Berryhill, M.S. Clinical Counselor/Biofeedback Therapist

bumpercarbiofeedback@gmail.com

Sharon Demorest, Health Coach, Nutritionist

healthygutsolutions@gmail.com

Jody Mohoff, CNWC, CST-D

https://cranialsacraltherapynow.com

Dr. Mark Kelley, Naturopathic Doctor, Lac, Three Rivers Natural Medicine

https://thehealthyplace.com

Dr. Matthew Schlechten, Naturopathic Doctor

drschlechten@gmail.com, (406) 546-8678

Heidi Kaminski, Exercise Physiology and Nutrition, Pilates

https://healthbyheidi.net

Anna Stephens, Pendulum Energy Dowsing

madukes8070@gmail.com

Sherry Quarnstrom, Author, Intuitive Guide, Personal Empowerment Coach

sherryq777@gmail.com

Christina Oss LaBang, Hospice RN and Author

'ANDEANsolrocks: Pathway of Light'

HeartMath Institute

https://heartmath.org

International Center for Reiki Training

https://reiki.org

As You Wish Publishing, Todd & Kyra Schaefer

https://asyouwishpublishing.com

AFTERWORD

As this book is in the final stages before getting sent off to my publisher, I am feeling into the now moment. I realize my path to physical healing was a walk unique to me and yet one that worked because I followed my intuition and listened to my body wisdom. I hope that is what you understood from my yearlong sojourn into wellness, that you too can seek internal wisdom, access strength and determine what is right for you. Be courageous. Claim your power. It really is up to you.

How is my health nearly 20 months after my diagnosis of stage 3 cancer? I continue to be cancer free but that does not mean I am resting on my laurels. I am very actively involved in taking action on a daily basis for my health profile. I commit to weekly appointments with my naturopath. I do infusions of nutritional support when needed. I take supplements several times a day based on my ever changing body needs. I eat healthier, drink more water and exercise regularly. I dance. I laugh and sing. I seek out new healing modalities and continue with the ones that resonate for me. My body is my temple and as such, deserves my continuous care and attention. Self-care is a sacred act and should not be overlooked or taken for granted.

As you probably well understand having come this far in the book, I view my body as an exquisite piece of my soul contract that, for the time being, needs to stay earthbound in order to fulfill that agreement. But for me, the spiritual side of my life is me, it is who I am and I remain steeped in the field of energy potential, getting more and more sensitive to the dance of frequency around me and within me.

It is not always easy to be so aware of the subtle realms. In fact, I was just sharing with Barbara the other morning, I was feeling the dying off of a species of bacteria in my body that needed to go away but of which I could feel the energy of death around. I sat in quiet contemplation while honoring the uninvited life force that was leaving, the life force that did not belong there but had been taking residence within me. Sometimes the awarenesses are so bizarre, I do not speak them to another soul except Jack. As such, I continue to navigate the waters of change within me, around me, and through the collective energies we all share.

To write a book is a labor of love. To be open and vulnerable to my truth and sharing it with the world is a level of compassionate action, understanding that maybe someone else on the planet may be helped by the exposure. To feel naked to the truth of me has taken courage and an honoring of my life unlike anything I've experienced before now.

I have the understanding this will be the last book I write so intimately with Jack. It pains me to know this part of our journey is coming to a close. Not that he is leaving me by any stretch, but our writing together in this way will shift. Writing will always be a part of my expression of life exploration, but our work together is transforming. Part of the reason I believe this is happening is I am going forward in living my life. I am here on this beautiful planet and ready to move into love again on the physical plane with another man who is here.

My heart is full to overflowing with the love of my divine beloved Jack, who will never leave me. I realize I will love again in the here and now, grounded in the physical, expressing through my body, feeling the love of another embodied soul who chooses to dance life with me. In this dance of life grounded on the planet, my body experiences healing and the desire to stay on the planet for as long as I am able. Making love is such a sacred and divine act between two souls who share each other's energy and I for one am ready to honor and accept that form of love into my reality. I will also love myself as fully as I can, filling this human vessel and soul with things that bring me joy.

My service to others through my work is a guarantee to my healing. God gifted me another chance to hold the light for others and I will not let the divinity within all-that-is down. I am but a humble servant to all souls who seek love, light, connection, and to help them know they are not alone.

This book is a testament to that commitment. Thank you for joining Jack and me on surfing the waves, falling into the deep, and breathing in the love we share with you.

ACKNOWLEDGEMENTS

How do I even begin to share with words my gratitude for LIFE? The gift of living I receive from God is beyond measure, time, and space into the realm of the living, breathing spirit. I am honored to be alive to share in this life with you. Thank you, God.

The soul I want to thank first and foremost is my beloved Jack. Without his constant participation in my life, things would have looked very different; I would not be the person I am today. Thank you, my love, for encouraging me, for writing with me, for being closer to me now than even in life while I evolve into another version of Becki here on the planet.

I want to thank my family for nursing my wounded body and soul back to health: my mom Kathleen, my dad Lionel from Spirit, my son TJ, my daughter Brandee and her husband Nate and their beautiful girls, Ada and Clara. You inspired me to stay the course with my healing journey. I extend a special thanks to my soul sister Barbara who was breathing every step with me along the way.

I also had many extended family members and friends step up to the plate to help me financially meet the building debt from all the various treatments. I could not have accomplished such amazing results had it not been for the ability to pursue what I knew I needed. Most of the alternative methods I describe are not covered by traditional health insurance. Thank you all for making it possible for me to choose my methods of healing. There are too many people to name but please know you are in my heart.

Numerous Health Practitioners and Energy Healers came forward to offer services free of charge and I am humbled by the generosity shown me in my time of need. Without hesitation, these people demonstrated what compassion-ate action means in real world application. I am forever humbled by your kind spirits.

I warmly acknowledge my health care team, from the medical doctors, to my naturopathic doctors, to all the alternative health care professionals assisting me. Your belief in me was crucial and I am happy I get to share some of your information in the resource list.

I never lost my inspiration while working with my amaz-ing clients. They may never know the depths of gratitude I have for being in service to them throughout my journey to health. By offering my soul to another's wellbeing, I was gifted healing through the sacred act of giving. They helped me remember why I am here and despite voicing my appreciation for them, I can never say enough about how precious the energy exchange with them was for my strength to walk the journey.

My friend Adele has taken my written word and helped me with editing all along the way. I could not have done this body of work without her continued support and encouragement. She was with me during some of my darkest moments. Thank you, dear friend, for holding me up when I could not hold myself.

Again, I want to thank Todd and Kyra Schaefer of As You Wish Publishing. Their dedication to the self-published author is commendable and I am so happy I get to go down the road of another book with your amazing team. Your vision is beautiful and your hearts are even greater.

My love goes out to the readers who have taken this year-long journey with me. I know at times it was intense and my sharing may have pushed buttons but what I know; it is in our connecting we grow, it is in our vulnerability we access strength, and it is in our humanness we experience divine love. You are now part of me and I a part of you. We are not separate but a group of souls ready to breathe deeply.

There are so many others who have impacted the writing of this book and, while the names are not mentioned, you know who you are. You helped me want to stay alive in this body for as long as I am gifted life. Thank you for helping me LOVE and LIVE!

Lastly, I am aware of Becki, the higher awareness who understands my soul's journey and who keeps breathing life into this form. Thank you for having the courage to write even when you knew it might trigger some readers. The open and raw truth of the year's experiences are now part of the fabric of the collective, available for others to read and understand.

We all have a story to share. We all hold the divine within us. We are enough and when we allow ourselves an open heart, the lifeblood of the sacred flows, taking us all into the realm of magic. Thank you for being part of mine.

ABOUT THE AUTHOR

Becki Koon

Heart Walker, Energy Dancer, Passion Promoter

Becki Koon is an International Bestselling Author and Speaker who is a Heart-based Energy Intuitive, Holy Fire III® Reiki Master, HeartMath® Coach, Life Coach, Theta-Healer, Crystal Practitioner, and ULC Minister. Through her business, Step Stone, Becki empowers people to seek their inner wisdom while holding space for them to heal, discover, and grow into the next highest version of themselves and she does this through compassionate love. She likes to refer to herself as the mid-wife of birthing a person's remembrance of their divine essence or purpose. Becki views her service in the world as a sacred offering to those she is fortunate to connect with.

Becki's work has evolved in a way she never expected. When her husband of 12 years passed, she knew her life was forever changed. What she did not expect was that she would wake up to the capability of communication with him through mediumship. Now, in Reiki and other healing sessions, Becki receives guidance from not only

Jack but her angelic guides and family of light, other people's guides, loved ones who have passed, and ascended masters. The world of channeling higher beings is a gift she says is a salve that has helped her deal with loss, grief, and her own health challenges.

Being in service to others has given Becki an outlet for the compassionate wisdom she gained. Conscious death, afterlife channeling, and self-love have changed her life, her work, her very essence, and she vows to continue using the gifts Jack so lovingly encouraged her to remember and offer to the world. The transition from physical body to soul essence need not be frightening but can be a beautiful honoring and celebration of LIFE and LOVE never-ending.

Contact:

stepstone2you@gmail.com
www.beckikoon.com
www.facebook.com/becki.koon.consulting
amazon.com/author/beckikoon